The ISIS Threat

The Rise of the Islamic State and their Dangerous Potential

Providence Research Publishing

2

Contents

Introduction

This collection of data from a variety of important sources brings to light the true threat of the so-called Islamic State. Information from military advisors, journalists, Congressional Hearings, and the President of the United States are compiled to provide a clear picture of ISIS' dangerous global potential.

"They have declared that they are at war with the United States....
They have a leader in Baghdadi. They have already conquered territory, about half of Iraq, about half of Syria....
They have made absolutely breathtaking strides in their short tenure of advancement. So they have land. They have a name. They have a leader. They have a government. It is known as shari'a law. That is Islamic law.....
They have an army. Twelve thousand, presumably, are in the Islamic State Army, and brutal they are--beheadings, women raped, men beheaded, innocent children shot in the head. It is absolutely devastating.
We see Christians have been chased out of the Middle East region......The Christians have been chased repeatedly out of Iraq. They are being chased out of the Baghdad area. They have been chased certainly out of northern Iraq and western Iraq, as Jews were chased out long ago. Now, in Syria, we hear the horrific stories of Christians who have been killed and murdered and beheaded simply because they name the name of Jesus Christ. Jews have been slaughtered and beheaded simply because they name the name of their God.
Is there any greater intolerance than the intolerance that has been shown repeatedly, brutally, lethally, by the Islamic State against Jews and Christians, and, yes, Muslims whom they disagree with."

- Congresswoman Michelle Bachman, 2014

Background of ISIL

The Islamic State, previously calling itself the Islamic State of Iraq and the Levant (ISIL) or the Islamic State of Iraq and Syria (ISIS) and also known by the Arabic acronym Daʿesh (داعش), is an unrecognized state and a Sunni jihadist group active in Iraq and Syria in the Middle East. In its self-proclaimed status as a caliphate, it claims religious authority over all Muslims across the world and aspires to bring most of the Muslim-inhabited regions of the world under its political control beginning with territory in the Levant region which includes Jordan, Israel, Palestine, Lebanon, Cyprus and part of southern Turkey.

The group has been described by the United Nations, Israel, the Philippines and Western and Middle Eastern media as a terrorist group and has been designated a foreign terrorist organization by the United States, the United Kingdom, Australia, Canada, Indonesia and Saudi Arabia. The United Nations and Amnesty International have accused the group of grave human rights abuses.

The Islamic State, also widely known as ISIS, ISIL and Daʿesh, originated as Jama'at al-Tawhid wal-Jihad in 1999. This group was the forerunner of Tanzim Qaidat al-Jihad fi Bilad al-Rafidayn—commonly known as al-Qaeda in Iraq(AQI)—a group formed by Abu Musab Al Zarqawi in 2004 which took part in the Iraqi insurgency against American-led forces and their Iraqi allies following the 2003 invasion of Iraq. During the 2003–2011 Iraq War, it joined other Sunni insurgent groups to form the Mujahideen Shura Council, which consolidated further into the Islamic State of Iraq (ISI) (/ˈaɪsɪ/) shortly afterwards. At its height it enjoyed a significant presence in the Iraqi governorates of Al Anbar, Nineveh,Kirkuk, most of Salah ad Din, parts of Babil, Diyala and Baghdad, and claimed Baqubah as a capital city. However, the violent attempts by the Islamic State of Iraq to govern its territory led to a backlash from Sunni Iraqis and other insurgent groups in around 2008 which helped to propel the Awakening movement and a temporary decline in the group.

As ISIS, the group grew significantly under the leadership of Abu Bakr al-Baghdadi, gaining support in Iraq as a result of alleged economic and political discrimination against Iraqi Sunnis. Then, after entering the Syrian Civil War, it established a large presence in the Syrian governorates of Ar-Raqqah, Idlib, Deir ez-Zor and Aleppo. In June 2014, it had at least 4,000 fighters in its ranks in Iraq. It has claimed responsibility for attacks on government and military targets and for attacks that killed thousands of civilians. In August 2014, the Syrian Observatory for Human Rights claimed that the number of fighters in the group had increased to 50,000 in Syria and 30,000 in Iraq, while the CIA estimated in September 2014 that in both countries it had between 20,000 and 31,500 fighters. ISIS had close links to al-Qaedauntil February 2014 when, after an eight-month power struggle, al-Qaeda cut all ties with the group, reportedly for its brutality and "notorious intractability".

The group's original aim was to establish an Islamic state in the Sunni-majority regions of Iraq, and following ISIS's involvement in the Syrian Civil War this expanded to include controlling Sunni-majority areas of Syria. A caliphate was proclaimed on 29 June 2014, Abu Bakr al-Baghdadi—now known as Amir al-Mu'minin Caliph Ibrahim—was named as its caliph, and the group was renamed the Islamic State.

Names

The group has had number of different names since it was formed, including some names that other groups use for it.

Index of names

- al-Dawlah ("the State")
- al-Dawlat al-Islāmīyah ("the Islamic State")
- AQI : Al-Qaeda in Iraq : Tanẓīm Qāʿidat al-Jihād fī Bilād al-Rāfidayn
- DAʿESH/Daʿesh (variously transliterated: DAISH/Daish, DAASH/Daash, DAESH/Daesh, DA'ASH/Da'ash, DAAS/Daas, DA'ISH/Da'ish, DĀ'ASH/Dā'ash, DAIISH/Daiish, based on the acronym:داعش)
- IS : Islamic State
- ISI : Islamic State of Iraq : Dawlat al-ʿIraq al-Islāmīyah
- ISIL : Islamic State of Iraq and the Levant
- ISIS : Islamic State of Iraq and al-Sham
- Islamic State (name since June 2014)
- JTJ : Jamāʿat al-Tawḥīd wa-al-Jihād : The Organization of Monotheism and Jihad
- Mujahideen Shura Council
- QSIS : Al-Qaeda Separatists in Iraq and Syria

History of names

The group was founded in early 1999 by Abu Musab al-Zarqawi under the name *Jamā'at al-Tawḥīd wa-al-Jihād*, "The Organization of Monotheism and Jihad" (JTJ).

In October 2004, al-Zarqawi swore loyalty to Osama bin Laden and changed the name of the group to *Tanẓīm Qā'idat al-Jihād fī Bilād al-Rāfidayn*, "The Organization of Jihad's Base in the Country of the Two Rivers" or "The Organization of Jihad's Base in Mesopotamia", more commonly known as "Al-Qaeda in Iraq" (AQI). Although the group has never called itself "Al-Qaeda in Iraq", this name has frequently been used to describe it through its various incarnations.

In January 2006, AQI merged with several smaller Iraqi insurgent groups under an umbrella organization called the "Mujahideen Shura Council". This was claimed to be little more than a media exercise and an attempt to give the group a more Iraqi flavour and perhaps to distance al-Qaeda from some of al-Zarqawi's tactical errors, notably the 2005 bombings by AQI of three hotels in Amman. Al-Zarqawi was killed in June 2006, after which the group's direction shifted again.

On 12 October 2006, the Mujahideen Shura Council joined four more insurgent factions and the representatives of a number of Iraqi Arab tribes, and together they swore the traditional Arab oath of allegiance known as *Ḥilf al-Muṭayyabīn* ("Oath of the Scented Ones"). During the ceremony, the participants swore to free Iraq's Sunnis from what they described as Shia and foreign oppression, and to further the name of Allah and restore Islam to glory.

On 13 October 2006, the establishment of the *Dawlat al-'Iraq al-Islāmīyah*, "Islamic State of Iraq" (ISI) was announced. A cabinet was formed and Abu Abdullah al-Rashid al-Baghdadi became ISI's figurehead emir, with the real power residing with the Egyptian Abu Ayyub al-Masri. The declaration was met with hostile criticism, not only from ISI's jihadist rivals in Iraq, but from leading jihadist ideologues outside the country. Al-Baghdadi and al-Masri were both killed in a US–Iraqi operation in April 2010. The next leader of the ISI was Abu Bakr al-Baghdadi, the current leader of ISIS.

On 8 April 2013, having expanded into Syria, the group adopted the name "Islamic State of Iraq and the Levant", also known as "Islamic State of Iraq and al-Sham." The name is abbreviated as ISIL or alternately ISIS. The final "S" in the acronym ISIS stems from the Arabic word *Shām* (or *Shaam*), which in the context of globaljihad—as in Jund al-Sham, for example— refers to the Levant or Greater Syria. ISIS was also known as *al-Dawlah* ("the State"), or *al-Dawlat al-Islāmīyah* ("the Islamic State"). These are short-forms of the name "Islamic State of Iraq and al-Sham" in Arabic. The name "Daʿesh" (pronounced "Daʔesh" and transliterated as "Dāʿesh") is used particularly by ISIS's detractors such as those in Syria. The term based on the Arabic letters, Dāl, ʾAlif, ʿAyn and Šīn(Shin), which form the acronym(داعش) of the Arabic name translated as, "the Islamic State of Iraq and the Levant" (*al-Dawla al-Islamiya fi Iraq wa ash-Sham*). The group considers the term derogatory and reportedly uses flogging as a punishment for people who use the acronym in ISIS-controlled areas.

On 14 May 2014, the United States Department of State announced its decision to use "Islamic State of Iraq and the Levant" (ISIL) as the group's primary name. Which of these acronyms should be used to designate the group, ISIL or ISIS, has been discussed by several commentators.

On 29 June 2014, the establishment of a new caliphate was announced, and the group formally changed its name to the "Islamic State" (IS).

In late August 2014, a leading Islamic authority Dar al-Ifta al-Misriyyah in Egypt advised Muslims to stop calling the group "Islamic State" and instead refer to it as "Al-Qaeda Separatists in Iraq and Syria" or "QSIS", because of the militant group's un-Islamic character.

Ideology and beliefs

ISIS is a Sunni extremist group that follows al-Qaeda's hard-line ideology and adheres to global jihadist principles. Like al-Qaeda and many other modern-day jihadist groups, ISIS emerged from the ideology of the Muslim Brotherhood, the world's first Islamist group dating back to the late 1920s in Egypt. ISIS follows an extreme anti-Western interpretation of Islam, promotes religious violence and regards those who do not agree with its interpretations as infidels or apostates. Concurrently, ISIS—now IS—aims to establish a Salafist-orientated Islamist state in Iraq, Syria and other parts of the Levant.

ISIS's ideology originates in the branch of modern Islam that aims to return to the early days of Islam, rejecting later "innovations" in the religion which it believes corrupt its original spirit. It condemns later caliphates and the Ottoman Empire for deviating from what it calls pure Islam and hence has been attempting to establish its own caliphate. However, some Sunni commentators, including Salafi and jihadi muftis such as Adnan al-Aroor and Abu Basir al-Tartusi, say that ISIS and related terrorist groups are not Sunnis, but modern-day Kharijites—Muslims who have stepped outside the mainstream of Islam—serving an imperial anti-Islamic agenda. Other critics of ISIS's brand of Sunni Islam include Salafists who previously publicly supported jihadist groups such as al-Qaeda, for example the Saudi government official Saleh Al-Fawzan who claims that ISIS is a creation of "Zionists, Crusaders and Safavids", and the Jordanian-Palestinian writer Abu Muhammad al-Maqdisi who was released from prison in Jordan in June 2014.

Salafists such as ISIS believe that only a legitimate authority can undertake the leadership of jihad, and that the first priority over other areas of combat, such as fighting non-Muslim countries, is the purification of Islamic society. For example, when it comes to the Israeli–Palestinian conflict, since ISIS regards the Palestinian Sunni group Hamas as apostates who have no legitimate authority to lead jihad, it regards fighting Hamas as the first step toward confrontation with Israel.

Goals

Since 2004, the group's goal has been the foundation of an Islamic state in
the Levant. Specifically, ISIS sought the establishment of a caliphate, a type
of Islamic state led by a group of religious authorities under a supreme
leader—caliph—who is believed to be the successor to Mohammed. In June
2014, ISIS published a document which it claimed linked ISIS's leader Abu
Bakr al-Baghdadi to the prophet. That same month, ISIS removed "Iraq and
the Levant" from its name and began to refer to itself as the Islamic State,
declaring the territory that it occupied in Iraq and Syria a new caliphate and
naming al-Baghdadi as its caliph. By declaring a caliphate, al-Baghdadi was
demanding the allegiance of all devout Muslims according to Islamic
jurisprudence—fiqh. ISIS has also stated: "The legality of all emirates,
groups, states and organizations becomes null by the expansion of the
khilafah's authority and arrival of its troops to their areas." ISIS thus rejects
the political divisions established by Western powers at the end of World
War I in the Sykes–Picot Agreement as it absorbs territory in Syria and Iraq.

Territorial claims

On 13 October 2006, the group announced the establishment of the Islamic State of Iraq, which claimed authority over the Iraqi governorates of Baghdad, Anbar, Diyala, Kirkuk, Salah al-Din, Nineveh and parts of Babil. Following the 2013 expansion of the group into Syria and the announcement of the Islamic State of Iraq and the Levant, the number of wilayah—provinces—which it claimed increased to 16. In addition to the seven Iraqi wilayah, the Syrian divisions, largely lying along existing provincial boundaries, are Al Barakah, Al Kheir, Ar-Raqqah, Al Badiya, Halab, Idlib, Hama, Damascus and the Coast. After taking control of both sides of the border in mid-2014, ISIS created a new province incorporating both Syrian territory around Albu Kamal and Iraqi territory around Qaim. This new wilayah was designated al-Furat. In Syria, ISIS's seat of power is in Ar-Raqqah Governorate. Top ISIS leaders, including Abu Bakr al-Baghdadi, are known to have visited its provincial capital, Ar-Raqqah.

Governance

British security expert Frank Gardner concluded that the group's prospects of maintaining control and rule were greater in 2014 than they had been in 2006. Despite being as brutal as before, ISIS has become "well entrenched" among the population and is not likely to be dislodged by ineffective Syrian or Iraqi forces. It has replaced corrupt governance with functioning locally-controlled authorities. Services have been restored and there are adequate supplies of water and oil. With Western-backed intervention being unlikely, the group will "continue to hold their ground" and rule an area "the size of Pennsylvania for the foreseeable future", he said.

Ar-Raqqah in Syria is the *de facto* capital of the Islamic State. It is said to be a "test case" or "show case" of ISIS governance. As of September 2014, governance in Ar-Raqqah is under the total control of ISIS, where it has rebuilt the structure of modern government in less than a year. Former government workers from the Assad regime maintain their jobs after pledging allegiance to ISIS. Institutions, restored and restructured, are providing services. The Ar-Raqqah dam continues to provide electricity and water. Foreign expertise supplements Syrian officials in running civilian institutions. Only the police and soldiers are ISIS fighters, who receive confiscated lodging previously owned by non-Sunnis and others who fled. Welfare services are provided, price controls established, and taxes imposed on the wealthy. Exporting oil from oilfields that it has captured brings in tens of millions of dollars. ISIS runs a soft power program in the areas under its control in Iraq and Syria, which includes social services, religious lectures and *da'wah*—proselytizing—to local populations. It also performs public services such as repairing roads and maintaining the electricity supply.

Analysis

After significant setbacks for the group during the latter stages of the coalition forces' presence in Iraq, by late 2012 it was thought to have renewed its strength and more than doubled the number of its members to about 2,500, and since its formation in April 2013, ISIS grew rapidly in strength and influence in Iraq and Syria. In June 2014, *The Economist* reported that "ISIS may have up to 6,000 fighters in Iraq and 3,000–5,000 in Syria, including perhaps 3,000 foreigners; nearly a thousand are reported to hail from Chechnya and perhaps 500 or so more from France, Britain and elsewhere in Europe". Chechen fighter Abu Omar al-Shishani, for example, was made commander of the northern sector of ISIS in Syria in 2013. According to *The New York Times*, among ISIS's foreign fighters there are more than 100 Americans.

Analysts have underlined the deliberate inflammation of sectarian conflict between Iraqi Shias and Sunnis during the Iraq War by various Sunni and Shia players as the root cause of ISIS's rise. The post-invasion policies of the international coalition forces have also been cited as a factor, with Fanar Haddad, a research fellow at the National University of Singapore's Middle East Institute, blaming the coalition forces during the Iraq War for "enshrining identity politics as the key marker of Iraqi politics".

By 2014, ISIS was increasingly being viewed as a militia rather than a terrorist group by some organizations. As major Iraqi cities fell to al-Baghdadi's cohorts in June, Jessica Lewis, a former US army intelligence officer at the Institute for the Study of War, described ISIS as "not a terrorism problem anymore", but rather "an army on the move in Iraq and Syria, and they are taking terrain. They have shadow governments in and around Baghdad, and they have an aspirational goal to govern. I don't know whether they want to control Baghdad, or if they want to destroy the functions of the Iraqi state, but either way the outcome will be disastrous for Iraq." Lewis has called ISIS "an advanced military leadership". She said, "They have incredible command and control and they have a sophisticated reporting mechanism from the field that can relay tactics and directives up and down the line. They are well-financed, and they have big sources of manpower, not just the foreign fighters, but also prisoner escapees." According to the Institute for the Study of War, ISIS's 2013 annual report reveals a metrics-driven military command, which is "a strong indication of a unified, coherent leadership structure that commands from the top down". Middle East Forum's Aymenn Jawad Al-Tamimi said, "They are highly skilled in urban guerrilla warfare while the new Iraqi Army simply lacks tactical competence." Seasoned observers point to systemic corruption within the Iraq Army, it being little more than a system of patronage, and have attributed to this its spectacular collapse as ISIS and its allies took over large swaths of Iraq in June 2014.

While officials fear ISIS may either inspire attacks in the United States by sympathizers or those returning after joining ISIS, American intelligence agencies find there is no immediate threat or specific plots. Defense Secretary Chuck Hagel sees an "imminent threat to every interest we have." Daniel Benjamin, former top counterterrorism adviser, derides such alarmist talk as a "farce" that panics the public.

Hillary Clinton has stated: "The failure to help build up a credible fighting force of the people who were the originators of the protests against Assad—there were Islamists, there were secularists, there was everything in the middle—the failure to do that left a big vacuum, which the jihadists have now filled."

Propaganda and social media

ISIS is also known for its effective use of propaganda. In November 2006, shortly after the creation of the Islamic State of Iraq, the group established the al-Furqan Institute for Media Production, which produces CDs, DVDs, posters, pamphlets, and web-related propaganda products. ISIS's main media outlet is the I'tisaam Media Foundation, which was formed in March 2013 and distributes through the Global Islamic Media Front (GIMF). In 2014, ISIS established the Al Hayat Media Center, which targets a Western audience and produces material in English, German, Russian and French. In 2014 it also launched the Ajnad Media Foundation, which releases jihadist audio chants.

In July 2014, ISIS began publishing a digital magazine called Dabiq in multiple languages, including English. According to the magazine, its name is taken from the town in northern Syria, which is mentioned in a hadith about Armageddon. Harleen K. Gambhir, of the Institute for the Study of War, found that while al-Qaeda in the Arabian Peninsula's Inspire magazine focused on encouraging its readers to carry out lone-wolf attacks on the West, Dabiq is more concerned with establishing the religious legitimacy of ISIS and its self-proclaimed caliphate, and encouraging Muslims to emigrate there.

ISIS's use of social media has been described by one expert as "probably more sophisticated than most US companies". It regularly takes advantage of social media, particularly Twitter, to distribute its message by organizing hashtag campaigns, encouraging Tweets on popular hashtags, and utilizing software applications that enable ISIS propaganda to be distributed to its supporters' accounts. Another comment is that "ISIS puts more emphasis on social media than other jihadi groups. ... They have a very coordinated social media presence." In August 2014, Twitter administrators shut down a number of accounts associated with ISIS. ISIS recreated and publicized new accounts the next day, which were also shut down by Twitter administrators. The group has attempted to branch out into alternative social media sites, such as Quitter, Friendica and Diaspora; Quitter and Friendica, however, almost immediately worked to remove ISIS's presence from their sites. ISIS released some special videos to influence Muslim youths in the Indian subcontinent. Reportedly two youths from Thane and four from Mumbai joined ISIS from India. After finding this to be a genuine report the Indian Government has introduced measures to stop youths joining ISIS. Four youths from Hyderabad were caught in Kolkata while flying to Syria to join ISIS.

On 19 August 2014, a propaganda video showing the beheading of US photojournalist James Foley was posted on the Internet. ISIS claimed that the killing had been carried out in revenge for the US bombing of ISIS targets. The video promised that a second captured US journalist Steven Sotloff would be killed next if the airstrikes continued. On 2 September 2014, ISIS released a video purportedly showing their beheading of Sotloff. In the video the executioner says, "I'm back, Obama, and I'm back because of your arrogant foreign policy towards the Islamic State, because of your insistence on continuing your bombings and on Mosul Dam, despite our serious warnings. So just as your missiles continue to strike our people, our knife will continue to strike the necks of your people." The next scene shows the same executioner holding the orange jumpsuit of another prisoner, and saying "We take this opportunity to warn those governments that enter this evil alliance of America against the Islamic State to back off and leave our people alone." On 13 September 2014, ISIS released another similar video purportedly depicting the beheading of David C. Haines, a British aid worker they had been holding hostage.

Finances

A study of 200 documents—personal letters, expense reports and membership rosters—captured from Al-Qaeda in Iraq and the Islamic State of Iraq was carried out by the RAND Corporation in 2014. It found that from 2005 until 2010, outside donations amounted to only 5% of the group's operating budgets, with the rest being raised within Iraq. In the time-period studied, cells were required to send up to 20% of the income generated from kidnapping, extortion rackets and other activities to the next level of the group's leadership. Higher-ranking commanders would then redistribute the funds to provincial or local cells that were in difficulties or needed money to conduct attacks. The records show that the Islamic State of Iraq was dependent on members from Mosul for cash, which the leadership used to provide additional funds to struggling militants in Diyala, Salahuddin and Baghdad.

In mid-2014, Iraqi intelligence extracted information from an ISIS operative which revealed that the organization had assets worth US$2 billion, making it the richest jihadist group in the world. About three quarters of this sum is said to be represented by assets seized after the group captured Mosul in June 2014; this includes possibly up to US$429 million looted from Mosul's central bank, along with additional millions and a large quantity of gold bullion stolen from a number of other banks in Mosul. However, doubt was later cast on whether ISIS was able to retrieve anywhere near that sum from the central bank, and even on whether the bank robberies had actually occurred.

ISIS has routinely practiced extortion, by demanding money from truck drivers and threatening to blow up businesses, for example. Robbing banks and gold shops has been another source of income. The group is widely reported as receiving funding from private donors in the Gulf states, and both Iran and Iraqi Prime Minister Nouri al-Maliki have accused Saudi Arabia and Qatar of funding ISIS, although there is reportedly no evidence that this is the case.

The group is also believed to receive considerable funds from its operations in Eastern Syria, where it has commandeered oilfields and engages in smuggling out raw materials and archaeological artifacts. ISIS also generates revenue from producing crude oil and selling electric power in northern Syria. Some of this electricity is reportedly sold back to the Syrian government.

Since 2012, ISIS has produced annual reports giving numerical information on its operations, somewhat in the style of corporate reports, seemingly in a bid to encourage potential donors.

Equipment

The most common weapons used against US and other Coalition forces during the Iraq insurgency were those taken from Saddam Hussein's weapon stockpiles around the country, these included AKM variant assault rifles, PK machine guns and RPG-7s. ISIS has been able to strengthen its military capability by capturing large quantities and varieties of weaponry during the Syrian Civil War and Post-US Iraq insurgency. These weapons seizures have improved the group's capacity to carry out successful subsequent operations and obtain more equipment. Weaponry that ISIS has reportedly captured and employed include SA-7 and Stinger surface-to-air missiles, M79 Osa, HJ-8 and AT-4 Spigot anti-tank weapons, Type 59 field guns and M198 howitzers, Humvees, T-54/55, T-72, and M1 Abrams main battle tanks, M1117 armored cars, truck mounted DShK guns, ZU-23-2 anti-aircraft guns, BM-21 Grad multiple rocket launchers and at least one Scud missile.

When ISIS captured Mosul Airport in June 2014, it seized a number of UH-60 Blackhawk helicopters and cargo planes that were stationed there. However, according to Peter Beaumont of *The Guardian*, it seemed unlikely that ISIS would be able to deploy them.

ISIS captured nuclear materials from Mosul University in July 2014. In a letter to UN Secretary-General Ban Ki-moon, Iraq's UN Ambassador Mohamed Ali Alhakim said that the materials had been kept at the university and "can be used in manufacturing weapons of mass destruction". Nuclear experts regarded the threat as insignificant. International Atomic Energy Agency spokeswoman Gill Tudor said that the seized materials were "low grade and would not present a significant safety, security or nuclear proliferation risk".

History

As *Jama'at al-Tawhid wal-Jihad, Al-Qaeda in Iraq* and *Mujahideen Shura Council* (1999-2005)

Main articles: Jama'at al-Tawhid wal-Jihad, Tanzim Qaidat al-Jihad fi Bilad al-Rafidayn and Mujahideen Shura Council

Following the 2003 US-led invasion of Iraq, the Jordanian Salafi Jihadist Abu Musab al-Zarqawi and his militant group Jama'at al-Tawhid wal-Jihad, founded in 1999, achieved notoriety in the early stages of the Iraq insurgency, by not just carrying out attacks on coalition forces but also conducting suicide attack on civilian targets and beheading hostages. Al-Zarqawi's group grew in strength and attracted more fighters, and in October 2004 it officially pledged allegiance to Osama bin Laden's al-Qaeda network, changing its name to Tanzim Qaidat al-Jihad fi Bilad al-Rafidayn (تنظيم قاعدة الجهاد في بلاد الرافدين, "Organization of Jihad's Base in Mesopotamia"), also known as Al-Qaeda in Iraq (AQI). Attacks by the group against civilians, the Iraqi Government and security forces continued to increase in the next two years—see list of major resistance attacks in Iraq. In a letter to al-Zarqawi in July 2005, Ayman al-Zawahiri outlined a four-stage plan to expand the Iraq War, which included expelling US forces from Iraq, establishing an Islamic authority—a caliphate—spreading the conflict to Iraq's secular neighbors, and engaging in the Arab–Israeli conflict.

On 7 June 2006, al-Zarqawi was killed in an American airstrike and was succeeded as AQI's leader by the Egyptian militant Abu Ayyub al-Masri. On 13 October 2006, the Mujahideen Shura Council (MSC), an umbrella organization of AQI and other insurgent groups, declared the establishment of the Islamic State of Iraq (ISI), comprising Iraq's six mostly Sunni Arab governorates, with Abu Omar al-Baghdadi being announced as the self-proclaimed state's Emir. Al-Masri was given the title of Minister of War within the ISI's ten-member cabinet. According to a study compiled by US intelligence agencies in early 2007, the ISI planned to seize power in the central and western areas of the country and turn it into a Sunni Islamic state.

As *Islamic State of Iraq* (2006–2013)

Strength and activity

In 2006, the State Department's Bureau of Intelligence and
Research estimated that Al-Qaeda in Iraq's core membership was "more than
1,000". These figures do not include the other six AQI-led Salafi groups in
the Islamic State of Iraq. In 2007, estimates of the group's strength ranged
from just 850 to several thousand full-time fighters. The group was said to
be suffering high manpower losses, including those from its many
"martyrdom" operations, but for a long time this appeared to have little
effect on its strength and capabilities, implying a constant flow of volunteers
from Iraq and abroad. However, Al-Qaeda in Iraq more than doubled in
strength, from 1,000 to 2,500 fighters, after the US withdrawal from Iraq in
late 2011.

In 2007, some observers and scholars suggested that the threat posed by
AQI was being exaggerated and that a "heavy focus on al-Qaeda obscures a
much more complicated situation on the ground". According to National
Intelligence Estimate and Defense Intelligence Agency reports in July 2007,
AQI accounted for 15% percent of attacks in Iraq. However, the
Congressional Research Service noted in its September 2007 report that
attacks from al-Qaeda were less than 2% of the violence in Iraq. It criticized
the Bush administration's statistics, noting that its false reporting of
insurgency attacks as AQI attacks had increased since the surge operations
began in 2007. In March 2007, the US-sponsored Radio Free Europe/Radio
Liberty analyzed AQI attacks for that month and concluded that the group
had taken credit for 43 out of 439 attacks on Iraqi security forces
and Shia militias, and 17 out of 357 attacks on US troops.

According to a US Government report in 2006, this group was most clearly
associated with foreign jihadist cells operating in Iraq and had specifically
targeted international forces and Iraqi citizens; most of Al-Qaeda in Iraq
(AQI)'s operatives were not Iraqi, but were coming through a series of safe
houses, the largest of which was on the Iraq–Syria border. AQI's operations
were predominately Iraq-based, but the United States Department of

State alleged that the group maintained an extensive logistical network throughout the Middle East, North Africa, South Asia and Europe. In a CNN special report in June 2008, Al-Qaeda in Iraq was called "a well-oiled ... organization ... almost as pedantically bureaucratic as was Saddam Hussein's Ba'ath Party", collecting new execution videos long after they stopped publicizing them, and having a network of spies even in the US military bases. According to the report, Iraqis—many of them former members of Hussein's secret services—were now effectively running Al-Qaeda in Iraq, with "foreign fighters' roles" seeming to be "mostly relegated to the cannon fodder of suicide attacks", although the organization's top leadership was still dominated by non-Iraqis.

Decline

The high-profile attacks linked to the group continued through early 2007, as AQI claimed responsibility for attacks such as the March assassination attempt on Sunni Deputy Prime Minister of Iraq Salam al-Zaubai, the April Iraqi Parliament bombing, and the May capture and subsequent execution of three American soldiers. Also in May, ISI leader al-Baghdadi was declared to have been killed in Baghdad, but his death was later denied by the insurgents; later, al-Baghdadi was even declared by the US to be non-existent. There were conflicting reports regarding the fate of al-Masri. From March to August, coalition forces fought the Battle of Baqubah as part of the largely successful attempts to wrest the Diyala Governorate from AQI-aligned forces. Through 2007, the majority of suicide bombings targeting civilians in Iraq were routinely identified by military and government sources as being the responsibility of al-Qaeda and its associated groups, even when there was no claim of responsibility, as was the case in the 2007 Yazidi communities bombings, which killed some 800 people in the deadliest terrorist attack in Iraq to date.

By late 2007, violent and indiscriminate attacks directed by rogue AQI elements against Iraqi civilians had severely damaged their image and caused loss of support among the population, thus isolating the group. In a major blow to AQI, many former Sunni militants who had previously fought alongside the group started to work with the American forces (see also below). The US troops surge supplied the military with more manpower for operations targeting the group, resulting in dozens of high-level AQI members being captured or killed. Al-Qaeda seemed to have lost its foothold in Iraq and appeared to be severely crippled. Accordingly, the bounty issued for al-Masri was eventually cut from $5 million to $100,000 in April 2008.

As of 2008, a series of US and Iraqi offensives managed to drive out the AQI-aligned insurgents from their former safe havens, such as the Diyala and Al Anbargovernorates and the embattled capital of Baghdad, to the area of the northern city of Mosul, the latest of the Iraq War's major battlegrounds. The struggle for control of Ninawa Governorate—the Ninawa campaign—was launched in January 2008 by US and Iraqi forces as part of the large-scale Operation Phantom Phoenix, which was aimed at combating al-Qaeda activity in and around Mosul, and finishing off the network's remnants in central Iraq that had escaped Operation Phantom Thunder in 2007. In Baghdad a pet market was bombed in February 2008 and a shopping centre was bombed in March 2008, killing at least 98 and 68 people respectively; AQI were the suspected perpetrators.

AQI has long raised money, running into tens of millions of dollars, from kidnappings for ransom, car theft—sometimes killing drivers in the process—hijacking fuel trucks and other activities. According to an April 2007 statement by their Islamic Army in Iraq rivals, AQI was demanding *jizya* tax and killing members of wealthy families when it was not paid. According to both US and Iraqi sources, in May 2008 AQI was stepping up its fundraising campaigns as its strictly militant capabilities were on the wane, with especially lucrative activity said to be oil operations centered on the industrial city of Bayji. According to US military intelligence sources, in 2008 the group resembled a "Mafia-esque criminal gang".

Conflicts with other groups

See also: Awakening movements in Iraq and Islamic Army-al-Qaeda conflict
The first reports of a split and even armed clashes between Al-Qaeda in Iraq
and other Sunni groups date back to 2005. In the summer of 2006, local
Sunni tribes and insurgent groups, including the prominent Islamist-
nationalist group Islamic Army in Iraq (IAI), began to speak of their
dissatisfaction with al-Qaeda and its tactics, openly criticizing the foreign
fighters for their deliberate targeting of Iraqi civilians. In September 2006,
30 Anbar tribes formed their own local alliance called the Anbar Salvation
Council (ASC), which was directed specifically at countering al-Qaeda-
allied terrorist forces in the province, and they openly sided with the
government and the US troops.

By the beginning of 2007, Sunni tribes and nationalist insurgents had begun
battling with their former allies in AQI in order to retake control of their
communities. In early 2007, forces allied to Al-Qaeda in Iraq committed a
series of attacks on Sunnis critical of the group, including the February 2007
attack in which scores of people were killed when a truck bomb exploded
near a Sunni mosque in Fallujah. Al-Qaeda supposedly played a role in the
assassination of the leader of the Anbar-based insurgent group 1920
Revolution Brigade, the military wing of the Islamic Resistance
Movement. In April 2007, the IAI spokesman accused the ISI of killing at
least 30 members of the IAI, as well as members of the Jamaat Ansar al-
Sunna and Mujahideen Army insurgent groups, and called on Osama bin
Laden to intervene personally to rein in Al-Qaeda in Iraq. The following
month, the government announced that AQI leader al-Masri had been killed
by ASC fighters. Four days later, AQI released an audio tape in which a
man claiming to be al-Masri warned Sunnis not to take part in the political
process; he also said that reports of internal fighting between Sunni militia
groups were "lies and fabrications". Later in May, the US forces announced
the release of dozens of Iraqis who were tortured by AQI as a part of the
group's intimidation campaign.

By June 2007, the growing hostility between foreign-influenced jihadists
and Sunni nationalists had led to open gun battles between the groups in

Baghdad. The Islamic Army soon reached a ceasefire agreement with AQI, but refused to sign on to the ISI. There were reports that Hamas of Iraq insurgents were involved in assisting US troops in their Diyala Governorate operations against Al-Qaeda in August 2007. In September 2007, AQI claimed responsibility for the assassination of three people including the prominent Sunni sheikh Abdul Sattar Abu Risha, leader of the Anbar "Awakening council". That same month, a suicide attack on a mosque in the city of Baqubah killed 28 people, including members of Hamas of Iraq and the 1920 Revolution Brigade, during a meeting at the mosque between tribal and guerilla leaders and the police. Meanwhile, the US military began arming moderate insurgent factions when they promised to fight Al-Qaeda in Iraq instead of the Americans.

By December 2007, the strength of the "Awakening" movement irregulars—also called "Concerned Local Citizens" and "Sons of Iraq"—was estimated at 65,000–80,000 fighters. Many of them were former insurgents, including alienated former AQI supporters, and they were now being armed and paid by the Americans specifically to combat al-Qaeda's presence in Iraq. As of July 2007, this highly controversial strategy proved to be effective in helping to secure the Sunni districts of Baghdad and the other hotspots of central Iraq, and to root out the al-Qaeda-aligned militants.

By 2008, the ISI was describing itself as being in a state of "extraordinary crisis", which was attributable to a number of factors, notably the Anbar Awakening.

Transformation and resurgence

In early 2009, US forces began pulling out of cities across the country, turning over the task of maintaining security to the Iraqi Army, the Iraqi Police Service and their paramilitary allies. Experts and many Iraqis were worried that in the absence of US soldiers the ISI might resurface and attempt mass-casualty attacks to destabilize the country. There was indeed a spike in the number of suicide attacks, and through mid- and late 2009, the ISI rebounded in strength and appeared to be launching a concerted effort to cripple the Iraqi government. During August and October 2009, the ISI

claimed responsibility for four bombings targeting five government
buildings in Baghdad, including attacks that killed 101 at the ministries of
Foreign Affairs and Finance in August and 155 at the Ministry of Justice
and Ministry of Municipalities and Public Works in September; these were
the deadliest attacks directed at the new government in more than six years
of war. These attacks represented a shift away from the group's previous
efforts to incite sectarian violence, although a series of suicide attacks in
April targeted mainly Iranian Shia pilgrims, killing 76, and in June,
a mosque bombing in Taza killed at least 73 Shias from the Turkmen ethnic
minority.

In late 2009, the commander of the US forces in Iraq, General Ray Odierno,
stated that the ISI "has transformed significantly in the last two years. What
once was dominated by foreign individuals has now become more and more
dominated by Iraqi citizens". Odierno's comments reinforced accusations by
the government of Nouri al-Maliki that al-Qaeda and ex-Ba'athists were
working together to undermine improved security and sabotage the
planned Iraqi parliamentary elections in 2010. On 18 April 2010, the ISI's
two top leaders, Abu Ayyub al-Masri and Abu Omar al-Baghdadi, were
killed in a joint US-Iraqi raid near Tikrit. In a press conference in June 2010,
General Odierno reported that 80% of the ISI's top 42 leaders, including
recruiters and financiers, had been killed or captured, with only eight
remaining at large. He said that they had been cut off from Al Qaeda's
leadership in Pakistan, and that improved intelligence had enabled the
successful mission in April that led to the killing of al-Masri and al-
Baghdadi; in addition, the number of attacks and casualty figures in Iraq for
the first five months of 2010 were the lowest since 2003. In May 2011, the
Islamic State of Iraq's "emir of Baghdad" Huthaifa al-Batawi, captured
during the crackdown after the 2010 Baghdad church attackin which 68
people died, was killed during an attempted prison break, during which an
Iraqi general and several others were also killed.

On 16 May 2010, Abu Bakr al-Baghdadi was appointed the new leader of
the Islamic State of Iraq; he had previously been the general supervisor of

the group's provincial sharia committees and a member of its senior consultative council. Al-Baghdadi replenished the group's leadership, many of whom had been killed or captured, by appointing
former Ba'athist military and intelligence officers who had served during the Saddam Hussein regime. These men, nearly all of whom had spent time imprisoned by American forces, came to make up about one-third of Baghdadi's top 25 commanders. One of them was a former Colonel, Samir al-Khlifawi, also known as Haji Bakr, who became the overall military commander in charge of overseeing the group's operations.

In July 2012, al-Baghdadi's first audio statement was released online. In this he announced that the group was returning to the former strongholds that US troops and their Sunni allies had driven them from prior to the withdrawal of US troops. He also declared the start of a new offensive in Iraq called *Breaking the Walls* which would focus on freeing members of the group held in Iraqi prisons. Violence in Iraq began to escalate that month, and in the following year the group carried out 24 waves of VBIED attacks and eight prison breaks. By July 2013, monthly fatalities had exceeded 1,000 for the first time since April 2008. The *Breaking the Walls* campaign culminated in July 2013, with the group carrying out simultaneous raids on Taji and Abu Ghraib prison, freeing more than 500 prisoners, many of them veterans of the Iraqi insurgency.

Abu Bakr al-Baghdadi was declared a Specially Designated Global Terrorist on 4 October 2011 by the US State Department, with an announced reward of US$10 million for information leading to his capture or death.

As *Islamic State of Iraq and the Levant* (2013–2014)

Declaration and dispute with al-Nusra Front

In March 2011, protests began in Syria against the government of Bashar al-Assad. In the following months, violence between demonstrators and security forces led to a gradual militarization of the conflict. In August 2011, Abu Bakr al-Baghdadi began sending Syrian and Iraqi ISI members, experienced in guerilla warfare, across the border into Syria to establish an organization inside the country. Led by a Syrian known as Abu Muhammad al-Jawlani, the group began to recruit fighters and establish cells throughout the country. On 23 January 2012, the group announced its formation as *Jabhat al-Nusra li Ahl as-Sham*—Jabhat al-Nusra—more commonly known as al-Nusra Front. Al-Nusra grew rapidly into a capable fighting force with popular support among Syrian opposition.

In April 2013, al-Baghdadi released an audio statement in which he announced that al-Nusra Front had been established, financed and supported by the Islamic State of Iraq and that the two groups were merging under the name "Islamic State of Iraq and Al-Sham". Al-Jawlani issued a statement denying the merger and complaining that neither he nor anyone else in al-Nusra's leadership had been consulted about it. In June 2013, Al Jazeera reported that it had obtained a letter written by al-Qaeda leader Ayman al-Zawahiri, addressed to both leaders, in which he ruled against the merger, and appointed an emissary to oversee relations between them to put an end to tensions. In the same month, al-Baghdadi released an audio message rejecting al-Zawahiri's ruling and declaring that the merger was going ahead. In October 2013, al-Zawahiri ordered the disbanding of ISIS, putting al-Nusra Front in charge of jihadist efforts in Syria, but al-Baghdadi contested al-Zawahiri's ruling on the basis of Islamic jurisprudence, and the group continued to operate in Syria. In February 2014, after an eight-month power struggle, al-Qaeda disavowed any relations with ISIS.

According to journalist Sarah Birke, there are "significant differences" between al-Nusra Front and ISIS. While al-Nusra actively calls for the overthrow of the Assad government, ISIS "tends to be more focused on establishing its own rule on conquered territory". ISIS is "far more ruthless" in building an Islamic state, "carrying out sectarian attacks and imposing sharia law immediately". While al-Nusra has a "large contingent of foreign fighters", it is seen as a home-grown group by many Syrians; by contrast, ISIS fighters have been described as "foreign 'occupiers'" by many Syrian refugees. It has a strong presence in central and northern Syria, where it has instituted sharia in a number of towns. The group reportedly controlled the four border towns of Atmeh, al-Bab, Azaz and Jarablus, allowing it to control the entrance and exit from Syria into Turkey. Foreign fighters in Syria include Russian-speaking jihadists who were part of Jaish al-Muhajireen wal-Ansar (JMA). In November 2013, the JMA's ethnic Chechen leader Abu Omar al-Shishani swore an oath of allegiance to al-Baghdadi; the group then split between those who followed al-Shishani in joining ISIS and those who continued to operate independently in the JMA under a new leadership.

In May 2014, al-Qaeda leader Ayman al-Zawahiri ordered al-Nusra Front to stop attacks on its rival ISIS. In June 2014, after continued fighting between the two groups, al-Nusra's branch in the Syrian town of al-Bukamal pledged allegiance to ISIS.

Conflicts with other groups

See also: Inter-rebel conflict during the Syrian Civil War

In Syria, rebels affiliated with the Islamic Front and the Free Syrian Army launched an offensive against ISIS militants in and around Aleppo in January 2014.

Relations with the Syrian government

In January 2014, *The Daily Telegraph* said that Western "intelligence sources" believed that the Syrian government made secret oil deals with ISIS and al-Nusra Front, alleging that the militants were funding their campaign by selling crude oil to the regime from the fields they have captured.

As *Islamic State* (2014–present)

On 29 June 2014, ISIS removed "Iraq and the Levant" from its name and began to refer to itself as the Islamic State, declaring the territory under its control a new caliphate and naming Abu Bakr al-Baghdadi as its caliph. On the first night of Ramadan, Shaykh Abu Muhammad al-Adnani al-Shami, spokesperson for ISIS, described the establishment of the caliphate as "a dream that lives in the depths of every Muslim believer" and "the abandoned obligation of the era". He said that the group's ruling Shura Council had decided to establish the caliphate formally and that Muslims around the world should now pledge their allegiance to the new caliph. The declaration of a caliphate has been criticized and ridiculed by Muslim scholars and rival Islamists inside and outside the occupied territory.

By that time, many moderate rebels had been assimilated into the group. In August 2014, a high-level IS commander said that "In the East of Syria, there is no Free Syrian Army any longer. All Free Syrian Army people have joined the Islamic State". The Islamic State had recruited more than 6,300 fighters in July 2014 alone, many of them coming from the Free Syrian Army.

Analysts observed that dropping the reference to region reflected a widening of the group's scope, and Laith Alkhouri, a terrorism analyst, thought that after capturing many areas in Syria and Iraq, ISIS felt this was a suitable opportunity to take control of the global jihadist movement.

A week before it changed its name to the Islamic State, ISIS had captured the Trabil crossing on the Jordan–Iraq border, the only border crossing between the two countries. ISIS has received some public support in Jordan, albeit limited, partly owing to state repression there. Raghad Hussein, the daughter of Saddam Hussein now living in opulent asylum in Jordan, has publicly expressed support for the advance of ISIS in Iraq, reflecting the Ba'athist alliance of convenience with ISIS with the goal of return to power in Bagdad. ISIS undertook a recruitment drive in Saudi Arabia where tribes in the north are linked to those in western Iraq and eastern Syria.

In June and July 2014, Jordan and Saudi Arabia moved their troops to the borders with Iraq after Iraq lost control of, or withdrew from, the strategic crossing points that came under the control of ISIS. There was speculation that al-Maliki had ordered a withdrawal of troops from the Iraq–Saudi crossings in order "to increase pressure on Saudi Arabia and bring the threat of Isis over-running its borders as well".

After the group captured Kurdish-controlled territory and massacred Yazidis, the US launched a humanitarian mission and aerial bombing campaign against ISIS.

In July 2014, Boko Haram leader Abubakar Shekau declared support for the new Calpihate and Caliph Ibrahim. In August, Shekau announced that Boko Haram had captured the Nigerian town of Gwoza. Shekau announced: "Thanks be to God who gave victory to our brethren in Gwoza and made it a state among the Islamic states". Boko Haram launched an offensive in Adamawa and Borno States in northeastern Nigeria in September, following the example of the Islamic State.

The moderate Free Syrian Army rebels have been backed by the United States with weapons and training. On 12 September 2014, the Western-backed Free Syrian Army and the Islamic State signed a "non-aggression" agreement. However, according to a Syrian National Coalition official, no Syrian opposition groups have entered a ceasefire agreement with ISIS.

Human rights abuses

In early September 2014, the United Nations Human Rights Council agreed to send a team to Iraq and Syria to investigate the abuses and killings being carried out by the Islamic State on "an unimaginable scale". Zeid Ra'ad al Hussein of Jordan, who has taken over Navi Pillay's post as the UN High Commissioner for Human Rights, urged world leaders to step in to protect women and children suffering at the hands of Islamic State militants, who he said were trying to create a "house of blood". He appealed to the international community to concentrate its efforts on ending the conflict in Iraq and Syria.

War crimes accusations

In July 2014, the BBC reported the United Nations' chief investigator as stating: "Fighters from the Islamic State in Iraq and the Levant (Isis) may be added to a list of war crimes suspects in Syria."

In August 2014, the United Nations accused the Islamic State of committing "mass atrocities" and war crimes.

Religious persecution

ISIS compels people in the areas it controls, under the penalty of death, torture or mutilation, to declare Islamic creed, and live according to its interpretation of Sunni Islam and sharia law. It directs violence against Shia Muslims,indigenous Assyrian, Chaldean, Syriac and Armenian Christians, Yazidis, Druze, Shabaks andMandeans in particular.

Amnesty International has accused ISIS of the ethnic cleansing of minority groups in northern Iraq.

Treatment of civilians

During the Iraqi conflict in 2014, ISIS released dozens of videos showing its ill treatment of civilians, many of whom had apparently been targeted on the basis of their religion or ethnicity. Navi Pillay, UN High Commissioner for Human Rights, warned of war crimes occurring in the Iraqi war zone, and disclosed one UN report of ISIS militants murdering Iraqi Army soldiers and 17 civilians in a single street in Mosul. The United Nations reported that in the 17 days from 5 to 22 June, ISIS killed more than 1,000 Iraqi civilians and injured more than 1,000. After ISIS released photographs of its fighters shooting scores of young men, the United Nations declared that cold-blooded "executions" said to have been carried out by militants in northern Iraq almost certainly amounted to war crimes.

ISIS's advance in Iraq in mid-2014 was accompanied by continuing violence in Syria. On 29 May, a village in Syria was raided by ISIS and at least 15 civilians were killed, including, according to Human Rights Watch, at least six children. A hospital in the area confirmed that it had received 15 bodies on the same day. The Syrian Observatory for Human Rights reported that on 1 June, a 102-year-old man was killed along with his whole family in a village in Hama.

ISIS has recruited to its ranks Iraqi children, who can be seen with masks on their faces and guns in their hands patrolling the streets of Mosul.

Sexual violence allegations

According to one report, ISIS's capture of Iraqi cities in June 2014 was accompanied by an upsurge in crimes against women, including kidnap and rape. *The Guardian* reported that ISIS's extremist agenda extended to women's bodies and that women living under their control were being captured and raped. Hannaa Edwar, a leading women's rights advocate in Baghdad who runs an NGO called Iraqi Al-Amal Association (IAA), said that none of her contacts in Mosul were able to confirm any cases of rape. However, another Baghdad-based women's rights activist, Basma al-Khateeb, said that a culture of violence existed in Iraq against women generally and felt sure that sexual violence against women was happening in Mosul involving not only ISIS but all armed groups.

During a meeting with Nouri al-Maliki, British Foreign Minister William Hague said with regard to ISIS: "Anyone glorifying, supporting or joining it should understand that they would be assisting a group responsible for kidnapping, torture, executions, rape and many other hideous crimes". According to Martin Williams in *The Citizen*, some hard-line Salafists apparently regard extramarital sex with multiple partners as a legitimate form of holy war and it is "difficult to reconcile this with a religion where some adherents insist that women must be covered from head to toe, with only a narrow slit for the eyes".

Haleh Esfandiari from the Woodrow Wilson International Center for Scholars has highlighted the abuse of local women by ISIS militants after they have captured an area. "They usually take the older women to a makeshift slave market and try to sell them. The younger girls ... are raped or married off to fighters", she said, adding, "It's based on temporary marriages, and once these fighters have had sex with these young girls, they just pass them on to other fighters." Yezidi girls in Iraq allegedly raped by ISIS fighters have committed suicide by jumping to their death from Mount Sinjar, as described in a witness statement.

Guidelines for civilians

After the self-proclaimed Islamic State captured cities in Iraq, ISIS issued guidelines on how to wear clothes and veils. ISIS warned women in the city of Mosul to wear full-face veils or face severe punishment. A cleric told Reuters in Mosul that ISIS gunmen had ordered him to read out the warning in his mosque when worshippers gathered. ISIS also banned naked mannequins and ordered the faces of both male and female mannequins to be covered. ISIS released 16 notes labeled "Contract of the City", a set of rules aimed at civilians in Nineveh. One rule stipulated that women should stay at home and not go outside unless necessary. Another rule said that stealing would be punished by amputation.

In addition to banning the sale and use of alcohol (which is customary in Muslim culture), militants have banned the sale and use of cigarettes and hookah pipes. They have also banned "music and songs in cars, at parties, in shops and in public, as well as photographs of people in shop windows."

Christians living in areas under ISIS control who wanted to remain in the "caliphate" faced three options: converting to Islam, paying a religious levy—jizya—or death. "We offer them three choices: Islam; the dhimma contract – involving payment of jizya; if they refuse this they will have nothing but the sword", ISIS said. ISIS had already set similar rules for Christians in Ar-Raqqah, Syria, once one of the nation's most liberal cities.

Timeline of events

2003–06 events

The Al-Askari Mosque, one of the holiest sites in Shia Islam, after the first attack by Al-Qaeda in Iraq in 2006

- The group was founded in 1999 and its first leader was the Jordanian militant Abu Musab al-Zarqawi, who declared allegiance to Osama bin Laden's al-Qaeda network on 17 October 2004. Foreign fighters from outside Iraq were thought to play a key role in its network. The group became a primary target of the Iraqi government and its foreign supporters, and attacks between these groups resulted in more than 1,000 deaths every year between 2004 and 2010.

- The Islamic State of Iraq made clear its belief that targeting civilians was an acceptable strategy and it has been responsible for thousands of civilian deaths since 2004. In September 2005, al-Zarqawi declared war on Shia Muslims and the group used bombings—especially suicide bombings in public places—massacres and executions to carry out terrorist attacks on Shia-dominated and mixed sectarian neighborhoods. Suicide attacks by the ISI also killed hundreds of Sunni civilians, which engendered widespread anger among Sunnis.

2007 events

- Between late 2006 and May 2007, the ISI brought the Dora neighborhood of southern Baghdad under its control. Numerous Christian families left, unwilling to pay the jizya tax. US efforts to drive out the ISI presence stalled in late June 2007, despite streets being walled off and the use of biometric identification technology. By November 2007, the ISI had been removed from Dora, and Assyrian churches could be re-opened. In 2007 alone the ISI killed around 2,000 civilians, making that year the most violent in its campaign against the civilian population of Iraq.

- 9 March: The Interior Ministry of Iraq said that Abu Omar al-Baghdadi had been captured in Baghdad, but it was later said that the person in question was not al-Baghdadi.

- 19 April: The organization announced that it had set up a provisional government termed "the first Islamic administration" of post-invasion Iraq. The "emirate" was stated to be headed by Abu Omar al-Baghdadi and his "cabinet" of ten "ministers".

Name (English transliteration) and notablepseudonyms	Post
Abu Omar al-Baghdadi d. 18 April 2010 Abu Bakr al-Baghdadi al-Husseini al-Qurashi (aka Abu Du'a)	Emir
Abu Abdullah al-Husseini al-Qurashi al-Baghdadi	Vice Emir
Abu Abdul Rahman al-Falahi	"First Minister" (Prime Minister)
Abu Hamza al-Muhajir (aka Abu Ayyub al-Masri) d. 18 April 2010 Al-Nasser Lideen Allah Abu Suleiman (akaNeaman Salman Mansour al Zaidi)	War
Abu Uthman al-Tamimi	Sharia affairs
Abu Bakr al-Jabouri (aka Muharib Abdul-Latif al-Jabouri) d. 1/2 May 2007	Public Relations
Abu Abdul Jabar al-Janabi	Security
Abu Muhammad al-Mashadani	Information
Abu Abdul Qadir al-Eissawi	Martyrs and Prisoners

	Affairs
Abu Ahmed al-Janabi	Oil
Mustafa al-A'araji	Agriculture and Fisheries
Abu Abdullah al-Zabadi	Health
Mohammed Khalil al-Badria	Education

The names listed above are all considered to be noms de guerre.

- 3 May: Iraqi sources claimed that Abu Omar al-Baghdadi had been killed a short time earlier. According to *The Long War Journal*, no evidence was provided to support this and US sources remained skeptical. The Islamic State of Iraq released a statement later that day which denied his death.

- 12 May: In what was apparently the same incident, it was announced that "Minister of Public Relations" Abu Bakr al-Jabouri had been killed on 12 May 2007 nearTaji. The exact circumstances of the incident remain unknown. The initial version of the events at Taji, as given by the Iraqi Interior Ministry, was that there had been a shoot-out between rival Sunni militias. Coalition and Iraqi government operations were apparently being conducted in the same area at about the same time and later sources implied that they were directly involved, with al-Jabouri being killed while resisting arrest. (See Abu Omar al-Baghdadi for details.)

- 12 May: The ISI issued a press release claiming responsibility for an ambush at Al Taqa, Babil on 12 May 2007, in which one Iraqi soldier and four US 10th Mountain Division soldiers were killed. Three soldiers of the US unit were captured and one was found dead in the Euphrates 11 days later. After a 4,000-man hunt by the US and allied forces ended without success, the ISI released a video in which it was claimed that the other two soldiers had been killed and buried, but no direct proof was given. Their bodies were found a year later.

- 18 June: The US launched Operation Arrowhead Ripper, as "a large-scale effort to eliminate Al-Qaeda in Iraq terrorists operating in Baquba and its surrounding areas". (See also Diyala province campaign.)

- 25 June: The suicide bombing of a meeting of Al Anbar tribal leaders and officials at Mansour Hotel, Baghdad killed 13 people, including six Sunni sheikhs and other prominent figures. This was proclaimed by the ISI to have been in retaliation for the rape of a Sunni woman by Iraqi police. Security at the hotel, which is 100 meters outside the Green Zone, was provided by a British contractor which had apparently hired guerrilla fighters to provide physical security. There were allegations that an Egyptian Islamist group may have been responsible for the bombing, but this has never been proven.

- In July, Abu Omar al-Baghdadi released an audio tape in which he issued an ultimatum to Iran. He said: "We are giving the Persians, and especially the rulers of Iran, a two-month period to end all kinds of support for the Iraqi Shia government and to stop direct and indirect intervention ... otherwise a severe war is waiting for you." He also warned Arab states against doing business with Iran. Iran supports the Iraqi government which many see as anti-Sunni.

- Resistance to coalition operations in Baqubah turned out to be less than anticipated. In early July, US Army sources suggested that any ISI leadership in the area had largely relocated elsewhere in early June 2007, before the start of Operation Arrowhead Ripper.

2009–12 events

- In the 25 October 2009 Baghdad bombings 155 people were killed and at least 721 were injured, and in the 8 December 2009 Baghdad bombings at least 127 people were killed and 448 were injured. The ISI claimed responsibility for both attacks.

- The ISI claimed responsibility for the 25 January 2010 Baghdad bombings that killed 41 people, and the 4 April 2010 Baghdad bombings that killed 42 people and injured 224. On 17 June 2010, the group claimed responsibility for an attack on the Central Bank of Iraq that killed 18 people and wounded 55. On 19 August 2010, in a statement posted on a website often used by Islamist radicals, the ISI claimed responsibility for the 17 August 2010 Baghdad bombings. It also claimed responsibility for the bombings in October 2010.

- According to the SITE Institute, the ISI claimed responsibility for the 2010 Baghdad church attack that took place during a Sunday Mass on 31 October 2010.

- 8 February 2011: According to the SITE Institute, a statement of support for Egyptian protesters—which appears to have been the first reaction of any group affiliated with al-Qaeda to the protests in Egypt during the 2011 Arab Spring Movement—was issued by the Islamic State of Iraq on jihadist forums. The message addressed to the protesters was that the "market of jihad" had opened in Egypt, that "the doors of martyrdom had opened", and that every able-bodied man must participate. It urged Egyptians to ignore the "ignorant deceiving ways" of secularism, democracy and "rotten pagan nationalism". "Your jihad", it went on, is in support of Islam and the weak and oppressed in Egypt, for "your people" in Gaza and Iraq, and "for every Muslim" who has been "touched by the oppression of the tyrant of Egypt and his masters in Washington and Tel Aviv".

- In a four-month process ending in October 2011, the Syrian government reportedly released imprisoned Islamic radicals and provided them with arms "in order to make itself the least bad choice for the international community."

- 23 July 2012: About 32 attacks occurred across Iraq, killing 116 people and wounding 299. The ISI claimed responsibility for the attacks, which took the form of bombings and shootings.

- In August 2012, two Iraqi refugees who have resided in Kentucky were accused of assisting AQI by sending funds and weapons; one has pleaded guilty.

2013 events

2012–14 Iraqi protests: Iraqi Sunni demonstrators protesting against the Shia-led government.

- Starting in April 2013, the group made rapid military gains in controlling large parts of Northern Syria, where the Syrian Observatory for Human Rights described them as "the strongest group".

- 11 May: Two car bombs exploded in the town of Reyhanlı in Hatay Province, Turkey. At least 51 people were killed and 140 injured in the attack. The attack was the deadliest single act of terrorism ever to take place on Turkish soil. Along with the Syrian intelligence service, ISIS was suspected of carrying out the bombing attack.

- By 12 May, nine Turkish citizens, who were alleged to have links with Syria's intelligence service, had been detained. On 21 May 2013, the Turkish authorities charged the prime suspect, according to the state-run Anatolia news agency. Four other suspects were also charged and 12 people had been charged in total. All suspects were Turkish nationals whom Ankara believed were backed by the Syrian government.

- In July, Free Syrian Army battalion chief Kamal Hamami—better known by his nom de guerre Abu Bassir Al-Jeblawi—was killed by the group's Coastal region emir after his convoy was stopped at an ISIS checkpoint in Latakia's rural northern highlands. Al-Jeblawi was traveling to visit the Al-Izz Bin Abdulsalam Brigade operating in the region when ISIS members refused his passage, resulting in an exchange of fire in which Al-Jeblawi received a fatal gunshot wound.

- Also in July, ISIS organised a mass break-out of its members being held in Iraq's Abu Ghraib prison. British newspaper *The Guardian* reported that over 500 prisoners escaped, including senior commanders of the group. ISIS issued an online statement claiming responsibility for the prison break, describing the operation as involving 12 car bombs, numerous suicide bombers and mortar and rocket fire. It was described as the culmination of a one-year campaign called "destroying the walls", which was launched on 21 July 2012 by ISIS leader Abu Bakr al-Baghdadi; the aim was to replenish the group's ranks with comrades released from the prison.

- In early August, ISIS led the final assault in the Siege of Menagh Air Base.

- In September, members of the group kidnapped and killed the Ahrar ash-Sham commander Abu Obeida Al-Binnishi, after he had intervened to protect members of a Malaysian Islamic charity; ISIS had mistaken their Malaysian flag for that of the United States.

- Also in September, ISIS overran the Syrian town of Azaz, taking it from an FSA-affiliated rebel brigade. ISIS members had attempted to kidnap a German doctor working in Azaz. In November 2013, *Today's Zaman*, an English-language newspaper in Turkey, reported that Turkish authorities were on high alert, with the authorities saying that they had detailed information on ISIS's plans to carry out suicide bombings in major cities in Turkey, using seven explosive-laden cars being constructed in Ar-Raqqah.

- From 30 September, several Turkish media websites reported that ISIS had accepted responsibility for the attack and had threatened further attacks on Turkey.

- In November, the Syrian Observatory for Human Rights stated: "ISIS is the strongest group in Northern Syria—100%—and anyone who tells you anything else is lying."

- In December, there were reports of fighting between ISIS and another Islamic rebel group, Ahrar ash-Sham, in the town of Maskana, Aleppo in Syria.

- In December, ISIS began an offensive in Anbar province in Iraq, changing insurgency there into a regional war which involved the United States and most of the states in the area.

2014 events

Some of the most recent events are transcluded below:

- 18 August: Pope Francis, leader of the world's 1.2 billion Roman Catholics, said that the international community would be justified in stopping Islamist militants in Iraq. He also said that it should not be up to a single nation to decide how to intervene in the conflict.

- 19 August: According to the Syrian Observatory for Human Rights, the Islamic State now has an army of more than 50,000 fighters in Syria. American journalist James Foley was beheaded by the Islamic State on video tape.

- 20 August: President Obama denounced the "brutal murder of Jim Foley by the terrorist group ISIL."

- 21 August: The US military admitted that a covert rescue attempt involving dozens of US Special Operations forces had been made to rescue James

Foley and other Americans held captive in Syria by Islamic State militants. The air and ground assault, involving the first known US military ground action inside Syria, had the authorization of President Obama. The ensuing gunfight resulted in one US soldier being injured. The rescue was unsuccessful, as Foley and the other captives were not in the location targeted. This was the first known engagement by US ground forces with suspected Islamic State militants. The US Defense Secretary warned that the Islamic State were tremendously well-funded, adding, "They have no standard of decency, of responsible human behavior", and that they were an imminent threat to the US.

- 22 August: The US is considering airstrikes on ISIS in Syria, which would draw US military forces directly into the Syrian Civil War, as President Obama develops a long-term strategy to defeat the Islamic State.
- 26 August: The Islamic State carried out a suicide attack in Baghdad killing 15 people and injuring 37 others.
- 28 August: The Islamic State beheaded a Lebanese Army soldier whom they had kidnapped. The group also beheaded a Kurdish Peshmerga fighter in response to Kurdistan's alliance with the United States, and executed around 250 Syrian soldiers captured after the fall of Tabqa Air Base in Ar-Raqqah province. The soldiers had earlier been marched to their place of execution wearing just their underwear.
- 29 August: UK Prime Minister David Cameron raised the UK's terror level to "severe" and committed to fight radical Islam "at home and abroad".
- 31 August: Iraqi military forces supported by Shia militias and American airstrikes broke the two-month siege of the northern Iraqi town of Amerli by Islamic State militants. German Federal Minister of Defence Ursula von der Leyen announced that Germany will send enough weapons to arm 4,000 Peshmerga fighters in northern Iraq fighting Islamic State insurgents. The delivery to be scheduled in stages will include 16,000 assault rifles, 40 machine guns, 240 rocket-propelled grenades, 500 MILAN anti-tank missiles with 30 launchers and 10,000 hand grenades, with a total value of around 70 million euros. In order to assess the needs of the Peshmerga and prevent an excessive accumulation of

arms, the Bundeswehr seconded six liaison officers to Erbil who will report to Berlin.

September 2014

- 1 September: The German government's Cabinet decision to arm the Kurdish Peshmerga militia was ratified in the Bundestag by a "vast majority" of votes, after an emotional debate.
- 2 September: The IS released a video showing the beheading of a man whom they identified as American journalist Steven Sotloff.
- 4 September: A member of the Islamic State issued a threat to Russian President Vladimir Putin, vowing to oust him over his support of Bashar al-Assad's regime in Syria.
- 5 September: The German Bundeswehr dispatched the first of a planned series of cargo planes to Iraq, loaded with helmets, vests, radios, and infrared night-vision rifle scopes. After a three-hour stopover in Baghdad for inspection, the aircraft will deliver the equipment to German personnel already in Erbil for distribution to the Kurdish fighters. Qassem Soleimani, Commander of the elite Iranian Revolutionary Guard Quds Force, has been to the Iraqi city of Amirli, to work with the United States in pushing back militants of the Islamic State.
- 8 September: The Islamic State carried out a double suicide attack in a town north of Baghdad killing 9 people and wounding 70 others.
- 10 September: After ISIS had outraged American opinion by beheading two American journalists and had seized control of large portions of Syria and Iraq in the face of ineffective opposition from American allies, President Obama decided on a new objective for a rollback policy in the Middle East. He announced: "America will lead a broad coalition to roll back this terrorist threat. Our objective is clear: We will degrade, and ultimately destroy, ISIL through a comprehensive and sustained counterterrorism strategy."
- 12 September: Western-backed Syrian rebels and the Islamic State signed a "non-aggression" agreement.
- 13 September: UK humanitarian aid worker David Cawthorne Haines, whose life had been threatened by Jihadi John in the Steven Sotloff video, was purportedly beheaded in a video titled "A Message to the Allies of America".

- 15 September: The Battle of Suq al Ghazi ended with a US–Iraqi win.
- 18 September: The Australian Federal Police, Australian Security Intelligence Organisation, Queensland Police and New South Wales Police launched the largest counterterrorism operation in Australian history. The targets were ISIS-linked networks thought to be planning to behead an Australian at home and launch mass-casualty attacks in populated areas. Fifteen people were arrested in the raids by police and intelligence organisations.

Administration of Barack Obama, 2014

Address to the Nation on United States Strategy To Combat the
Islamic State of Iraq and the Levant Terrorist Organization (ISIL)

September 10, 2014

My fellow Americans, tonight I want to speak to you about what the United States will do with our friends and allies to degrade and ultimately destroy the terrorist group known as ISIL.

As Commander in Chief, my highest priority is the security of the American people. Over the last several years, we have consistently taken the fight to terrorists who threaten our country. We took out Usama bin Laden and much of Al Qaida's leadership in Afghanistan and Pakistan. We've targeted Al Qaida's affiliate in Yemen and recently eliminated the top commander of its affiliate in Somalia. We've done so while bringing more than 140,000 American troops home from Iraq and drawing down our forces in Afghanistan, where our combat mission will end later this year. Thanks to our military and counterterrorism professionals, America is safer.

Still, we continue to face a terrorist threat. We can't erase every trace of evil from the world, and small groups of killers have the capacity to do great harm. That was the case before 9/11, and that remains true today. And that's why we must remain vigilant as threats emerge. At this moment, the greatest threats come from the Middle East and North Africa, where radical groups exploit grievances for their own gain. And one of those groups is ISIL, which calls itself the "Islamic State."

Now, let's make two things clear: ISIL is not Islamic. No religion condones the killing of innocents. And the vast majority of ISIL's victims have been Muslim. And ISIL is certainly not a state. It was formerly Al Qaida's affiliate in Iraq and has taken advantage of sectarian strife and Syria's civil war to gain territory on both sides of the Iraq-Syrian border. It is recognized by no government, nor by the people it subjugates. ISIL is a terrorist organization, pure and simple. And it has no vision other than the slaughter of all who stand in its way.

In a region that has known so much bloodshed, these terrorists are unique in their brutality. They execute captured prisoners. They kill children. They enslave, rape, and force women into marriage. They threatened a religious minority with genocide. And in acts of barbarism, they took the lives of two American journalists, Jim Foley and Steven Sotloff.

So ISIL poses a threat to the people of Iraq and Syria and the broader Middle East, including American citizens, personnel, and facilities. If left unchecked, these terrorists could pose a growing threat beyond that region, including to the United States. While we have not yet detected specific plotting against our homeland, ISIL leaders have threatened America and our allies. Our intelligence community believes that thousands of foreigners, including Europeans and some Americans, have joined them in Syria and Iraq. Trained and battle-hardened, these fighters could try to return to their home countries and carry out deadly attacks.

I know many Americans are concerned about these threats. Tonight I want you to know that the United States of America is meeting them with strength and resolve. Last month, I ordered our military to take targeted action against ISIL to stop its advances. Since then, we've conducted more than 150 successful airstrikes in Iraq. These strikes have protected American personnel and facilities, killed ISIL fighters, destroyed weapons, and given space for Iraqi and 2 Kurdish forces to reclaim key territory. These strikes have also helped save the lives of thousands of innocent men, women, and children.

But this is not our fight alone. American power can make a decisive difference, but we cannot do for Iraqis what they must do for themselves, nor can we take the place of Arab partners in securing their region. And that's why I've insisted that additional U.S. action depended upon Iraqis forming an inclusive Government, which they have now done in recent days. So tonight, with a new Iraqi Government in place, and following consultations with allies abroad and Congress at home, I can announce that America will lead a broad coalition to roll back this terrorist threat.

Our objective is clear: We will degrade and ultimately destroy ISIL through a comprehensive and sustained counterterrorism strategy.

First, we will conduct a systematic campaign of airstrikes against these terrorists. Working with the Iraqi Government, we will expand our efforts beyond protecting our own people and humanitarian missions so that we're hitting ISIL targets as Iraqi forces go on offense. Moreover, I have made it clear that we will hunt down terrorists who threaten our country, wherever they are. That means I will not hesitate to take action against ISIL in Syria, as well as Iraq. This is a core principle of my Presidency: If you threaten America, you will find no safe haven.

Second, we will increase our support to forces fighting these terrorists on the ground. In June, I deployed several hundred American service members to Iraq to assess how we can best support Iraqi security forces. Now that those teams have completed their work and Iraq has formed a Government, we will send an additional 475 service members to Iraq. As I have said before, these American forces will not have a combat mission. We will not get dragged into another ground war in Iraq. But they are needed to support Iraqi and Kurdish forces with training, intelligence, and equipment. We'll also support Iraq's efforts to stand up national guard units to help Sunni communities secure their own freedom from ISIL's control.

Across the border, in Syria, we have ramped up our military assistance to the Syrian opposition. Tonight I call on Congress again to give us additional authorities and resources to train and equip these fighters. In the fight against ISIL, we cannot rely on an Asad regime that terrorizes its own people, a regime that will never regain the legitimacy it has lost. Instead, we must strengthen the opposition as the best counterweight to extremists like ISIL, while pursuing the political solution necessary to solve Syria's crisis once and for all.

Third, we will continue to draw on our substantial counterterrorism capabilities to prevent ISIL attacks. Working with our partners, we will redouble our efforts to cut off its funding, improve our intelligence, strengthen our defenses, counter its warped ideology, and stem the flow of foreign fighters into and out of the Middle East. And in 2 weeks, I will chair a meeting of the U.N. Security Council to further mobilize the international community around this effort.

Fourth, we will continue to provide humanitarian assistance to innocent civilians who have been displaced by this terrorist organization. This includes Sunni and Shia Muslims who are at grave risk, as well as tens of thousands of Christians and other religious minorities. We cannot allow these communities to be driven from their ancient homelands.

So this is our strategy. And in each of these four parts of our strategy, America will be joined by a broad coalition of partners. Already, allies are flying planes with us over Iraq, sending arms and assistance to Iraqi security forces and the Syrian opposition, sharing intelligence, and providing billions of dollars in humanitarian aid. Secretary Kerry was in Iraq today meeting with the new Government and supporting their efforts to promote unity. And in the coming days, he will travel across the Middle East and Europe to enlist more partners in this fight, especially Arab nations who can help mobilize Sunni communities in Iraq and Syria to drive these terrorists from their lands. This is American leadership at its best: We stand with people who fight for their own freedom, and we rally other nations on behalf of our common security and common humanity.

My administration has also secured bipartisan support for this approach here at home. I have the authority to address the threat from ISIL, but I believe we are strongest as a nation when the President and Congress work together. So I welcome congressional support for this effort in order to show the world that Americans are united in confronting this danger.

Now, it will take time to eradicate a cancer like ISIL. And any time we take military action, there are risks involved, especially to the service men and women who carry out these missions. But I want the American people to understand how this effort will be different from the wars in Iraq and Afghanistan. It will not involve American combat troops fighting on foreign soil. This counterterrorism campaign will be waged through a steady, relentless effort to take out ISIL wherever they exist, using our air power and our support for partners' forces on the ground. This strategy of taking out terrorists who threaten us while supporting partners on the front lines is one that we have successfully pursued in Yemen and Somalia for years. And it is consistent with the approach I outlined earlier this year: to use force against anyone who threatens America's core interests, but to mobilize partners wherever possible to address broader challenges to international order.

My fellow Americans, we live in a time of great change. Tomorrow marks 13 years since our country was attacked. Next week marks 6 years since our economy suffered its worst setback since the Great Depression. Yet, despite these shocks, through the pain we've felt and the grueling work required to bounce back, America is better positioned today to seize the future than any other nation on Earth.

Our technology companies and universities are unmatched. Our manufacturing and auto industries are thriving. Energy independence is closer than it's been in decades. For all the work that remains, our businesses are in the longest uninterrupted stretch of job creation in our history. Despite all the divisions and discord within our democracy, I see the grit and determination and common goodness of the American people every single day, and that makes me more confident than ever about our country's future.

Abroad, American leadership is the one constant in an uncertain world. It is America that has the capacity and the will to mobilize the world against terrorists. It is America that has rallied the world against Russian aggression and in support of the Ukrainian peoples' right to determine their own destiny. It is America—our scientists, our doctors, our know-how—that can help contain and cure the outbreak of Ebola. It is America that helped remove and destroy Syria's declared chemical weapons so that they can't pose a threat to the Syrian people or the world again. And it is America that is helping Muslim communities around the world not just in the fight against terrorism, but in the fight for opportunity and tolerance and a more hopeful future.

America, our endless blessings bestow an enduring burden. But as Americans, we welcome our responsibility to lead. From Europe to Asia, from the far reaches of Africa to war-torn capitals of the Middle East, we stand for freedom, for justice, for dignity. These are values that have guided our Nation since its founding.

Tonight I ask for your support in carrying that leadership forward. I do so as a Commander in Chief who could not be prouder of our men and women in uniform: pilots who bravely fly in the face of danger above the Middle East and servicemembers who support our partners on the ground.

When we helped to prevent the massacre of civilians trapped on a distant mountain, here's what one of them said: "We owe our American friends our lives. Our children will always remember that there was someone who felt our struggle and made a long journey to protect innocent people."

That is the difference we make in the world. And our own safety, our own security, depends upon our willingness to do what it takes to defend this Nation and uphold the values that we stand for, timeless ideals that will endure long after those who offer only hate and destruction have been vanquished from the Earth.

May God bless our troops, and may God bless the United States of America.
NOTE: The President spoke at 9:01 p.m. on the State Floor at the White House. In his remarks, he referred to Ahmed Abdi Godane, leader of the al-Shabaab terrorist organization, who was killed by a U.S. airstrike in southern Somalia on September 1; and President Bashar al-Asad of Syria.

ISLAMIC JIHAD
Congresswoman Michelle Bachman's Speech - September 17, 2014

The SPEAKER pro tempore. Under the Speaker's announced policy of January 3, 2013, the gentlewoman from Minnesota (Mrs. Bachmann) is recognized for 60 minutes as the designee of the majority leader.

Mrs. BACHMANN. Mr. Speaker, I expect that, shortly, a colleague will be here that I will hand off to for a few minutes to deal with several housekeeping issues, but, for the moment that I have, I want to focus on an issue that has gained the attention--as well it should--of the American people.

The number one duty of government, Mr. Speaker, is to secure the safety and the security of the American people. That is why we have a government. That is why we exist. It is the reason why countries enjoy sovereignty and declare themselves sovereign nations.

That means they are a separate political unit, and they exist for the purpose of preserving the safety and security of their people. That is our duty, and that is our government.

It seems, Mr. Speaker, throughout each generation that somehow, some way, there is a force that comes against a nation. In different eras, we have had different foes that the United States has had to contend with, beginning at our founding, when the United States of America, through our Declaration of Independence and through our Constitution, on this, our Constitution Day--and, by the way, we say happy Constitution Day to all Americans. We are very proud of our United States Constitution.

Contained within the Constitution is the admonition to the President, to the Congress, to the Supreme Court, again, to ensure that, in our founding document, we understand that it is the duty of the government to secure the safety and the security of the American people.

What led up to the writing of the Declaration of Independence and to the American Revolution and, ultimately, to America's founding document with the United States Constitution was a reaction of the colonists against a great totalitarian oppression that was coming against the United States. That was from the British motherland of which the United States was a colony of.

We pushed back against that oppression for many and sundry reasons, some of which were taxation, others were the taking away the rights of

American citizens, whether it was forcing American citizens to take soldiers into their homes or taking away their rights as free men under the Magna Carta.

The American people rose up, and they said, ``We want to have freedom." They threw off the chains of the totalitarianism of the day, the British Empire.

Going further into the future with the War of 1812, again, the United States was pushed into a conflict with the British, and, again, we had to throw off that enemy. Again, we saw our own house come apart in the time of the Civil War. There was also the Spanish-American War.

The United States was engaged in a great totalitarianism in 1917 with World War I and, again, in World War II. There was a conflict in the totalitarianism of our day. It was an evil known as Communism, both from the Soviet threat and also from Nazism.

The United States came together as a Nation. We threw off the yoke of the oppressor, of the totalitarianism of our day--in other words, a regime that had an idea that it wanted to conquer the world with its evil and immoral philosophy, whether it was Communism or whether it was Nazism.

It seems, Mr. Speaker, that every generation is confronted by a great evil, and the moral questions of the day are related to that evil. The evil, Mr. Speaker, that we are dealing with today is something known as Islamic jihad.

Its face is ugly. Its face has reared not only just in recent decades and just the last few months of this summer, but Islamic jihad is something that has been around as long as the inception of Islam itself.

The regime of jihad has been defeated, summarily, time and time again throughout history, but it was defeated through military might, it wasn't defeated through diplomacy, and defeated it was.

It was defeated at Tours; it was defeated at the battle of the gates of Vienna; it was defeated again with the collapse of the Ottoman Empire in the 1920s; but it was defeated militarily. It was an idea that had grisly consequences. Those consequences were ones that led to bloodshed and suffering and misery for thousands of people across the world. Today is no different.

Today, we see the same level of bloodshed across the world. That bloodshed is coming to us, again, at the tip of the sword. This summer, it is known as the Islamic State. Some people know it as ISIS. Some people know it by the name ISIL. The President uses the term ``ISIL.''

This organization is just a continuation of al Qaeda--and a continuation of something even greater than al Qaeda--and that is the concept known as Islamic jihad.

Baghdadi, the head of the Islamic State, initially called them ISIS, which means the Islamic State of Iraq and al-Sham, or Syria. That was the territory that Baghdadi was seeking to conquer. He did, in fact, conquer much of that territory.

Then he changed the name of his organization to ISIL, the Islamic State in the Levant. The Levant is a geographical area that is greater than Syria and Iraq. It would comprise much of eastern Turkey, Israel, Gaza, Lebanon, and so forth, the greater area, if you will, of the central Mediterranean area.

After that, the Islamic State issued yet another press release with yet another name change. And in the course of that name change, the Islamic State decided to drop the IS and the IL, and now they are known simply as the Islamic State.

That is because the ambitions, Mr. Speaker, of Baghdadi and the Islamic State are far grander than just Iraq or just Syria or just eastern Turkey or Israel or Lebanon or Jordan or Gaza--far bigger.

The Islamic State, you see, Mr. Speaker, encompasses the entire globe, the planet Earth. Every part of this Earth, you see, Mr. Speaker, is what is intended. It is the ultimate in totalitarianism--what the Communists planned for, which was for control of the world under the umbrella of communism, and saw themselves ultimately defeated militarily; and again, what the Nazis saw, Mr. Speaker, as control of the world, national socialism through the Nazi Party movement and, ultimately, were defeated militarily.

So too, Mr. Speaker, the Islamic State sees their evil, violent, cruel, bloody philosophy also would encompass the Earth. That would include the United States of America. That would include, obviously, our great ally Israel. It would encompass all of North America. It would also cover the Asian nations. The entire world now, Mr. Speaker, is at threat from this totalitarianism.

And often it is said, never despise small beginnings. It is breathtaking, Mr. Speaker, what we have seen accomplished by the Islamic State. The leader, again, is a man named Baghdadi.

Baghdadi was a part of the franchise known as al Qaeda in Iraq. Al Qaeda began--we know about Osama bin Laden. Well, an affiliate of Osama bin Laden was the man named Baghdadi, who is the current head of the Islamic State.

Baghdadi, when he was a part of the franchise, al Qaeda in Iraq, was number three. We were able to target and kill number one and number two in the power structure in Iraq. That left Baghdadi as the next in command.

Baghdadi decided not only did he want to be the leader of al Qaeda in Iraq, he wanted so much more. But, you see, Baghdadi was waylaid for a period of time in his life. Why? Because Baghdadi was captured by the United States. He was found to be a terrorist. He was held in detention in Camp Baka in Iraq.

So we had him, the leader of the Islamic State, the organization responsible for the beheadings of Americans, the American photojournalist James Foley and the American photojournalist James Sotloff and, this Saturday, the beheading of another British journalist. Baghdadi is responsible for all of that and so much more.

Baghdadi was responsible for ordering the murdering of literally hundreds and thousands of individuals in Iraq. We saw Baghdadi line up hundreds of soldiers in Iraq, Iraqi soldiers, and they were brutally and mercilessly murdered, being shot in the back.

We also saw additional beheadings occur, and we saw also as they chased the Yazidis up Mount Sinjar. We also heard the horrific tales of how the merciless Islamic State literally stooped so low that they buried alive women and children in graves in August.

Mr. Speaker, I despise being as graphic as I am, but we must be face-to-face with the facts that we are facing. This is an evil regime. It is an evil philosophy with an evil goal. They are as equally committed to killing Jews as they are committed to killing Christians as they are committed to killing any Muslim who doesn't agree with their sick, failed philosophy.

The other thing we need to recognize, Mr. Speaker, is that this has a religious motivation, not because I say so, but because Baghdadi and the terrorists of the Islamic State say so. Their motivation is their religion. They say it is Islam that drives them to do what they are doing.

That is why it is perplexing, Mr. Speaker, that a week ago the President of the United States said in a televised address that Islam has nothing to do with the Islamic State. He said there are two fallacies of the Islamic State. Number one, he said, it is not Islam.

Well, Mr. President, you may not think it is Islam, but ask the leaders of

Islamic jihad what they think it is. They say forthrightly and boldly, with everything that is within them, that their motivation for beheading individuals, for burying women and children alive, for establishing a global power to enforce their sick, religious ideas upon the world is based upon their religion of Islam.

That is their reasoning, Mr. Speaker, out of their mouths. And I believe that it is prudent and wise to listen to the enemy, to find out what their motivations are.

We look no further than the mad, evil, maniacal leader of the Nazi Party, as he was rising in the 1930s, when he wrote his book called ``Mein Kampf." In his book, ``Mein Kampf," he wrote his detailed plan. You see, he wasn't being secret, Mr. Speaker, about the evil that he wanted to bring against the Jewish people. He was very forthright. The same can be said, Mr. Speaker, of Baghdadi, who is the head of the evil regime and ideology known as the Islamic State. Baghdadi.

As a matter of fact, Mr. Speaker, this is what the leader of the Islamic State had to say. This is in January, and he said this to the United States, and I quote. In a speech in January of this year, Baghdadi said to the United States: ``Soon we will be in direct confrontation. So watch out for us for we are with you, watching."

I repeat: ``Soon we will be in direct confrontation," meaning with the United States. ``So watch out for us for we are with you, watching."

That tells me, Mr. Speaker, that Baghdadi and the Islamic State don't intend to confine their bloodletting just in Iraq and Syria or in Jordan or Lebanon. Their designs are for the United States as well.

We have been told and we have read that there is an enormous amount of so-called chatter through the social media by members of the Islamic State and those who promote Islamic jihad to enter into the United States and to bring about atrocities here within the confines of our American sovereign soil.

You see, our sovereign soil has been invaded. Our sovereign soil was invaded at Benghazi. Our U.S. consulate in Benghazi when Ambassador Chris Stevens lost his life was U.S. soil. Islamic jihadists entered our sovereign soil and killed our U.S. Ambassador on that sovereign soil.

Just within a month or so ago, Islamic jihadists again took over the airport in Baghdad, and again we saw an embassy in Libya, in Tripoli, abandoned. So United States personnel were forced to flee the United States

Embassy in Tripoli and leave and gain escape through Tunisia.

It is really quite sobering when you think of the advances of Islamic jihad in the region. And that is why I don't understand, Mr. Speaker, I don't understand the thinking of the President when it is coming against this evil. I don't understand it because, you see, the Islamic State has not only declared their intention, they have declared that they are at war with the United States. They have declared they are at war. They have declared that they are a caliphate. They are a government. They are an Islamic government.

They have a leader in Baghdadi. They have already conquered territory, about half of Iraq, about half of Syria, which they control, also other parts of the Middle East as well. They also control parts of northern Lebanon.

They have made absolutely breathtaking strides in their short tenure of advancement. So they have land. They have a name. They have a leader. They have a government. It is known as shari'a law. That is Islamic law. That is their law of the land.

They also have an administration. They have a Shura Council, and they have an administration. They already have a line of hierarchy and an organizational flowchart of how they are going to run the Islamic State.

They have an army. Twelve thousand, presumably, are in the Islamic State Army, and brutal they are--beheadings, women raped, men beheaded, innocent children shot in the head. It is absolutely devastating.

We see Christians have been chased out of the Middle East region. The numbers are so dramatic, Mr. Speaker, of Christians that have had to flee Iraq, Christians in Mosul that have lived safely there. The ancient town of Nineveh, which Jonah went to preach in Nineveh, and that town is Mosul, Christians have been in Mosul since the time of Christ, 2,000 years. Mosul no longer has Christians. They were chased out of that city.

The Christians have been chased repeatedly out of Iraq. They are being chased out of the Baghdad area. They have been chased certainly out of northern Iraq and western Iraq, as Jews were chased out long ago.

Now, in Syria, we hear the horrific stories of Christians who have been killed and murdered and beheaded simply because they name the name of Jesus Christ. Jews have been slaughtered and beheaded simply because they name the name of their God.

Is there any greater intolerance, Mr. Speaker than the intolerance that has been shown repeatedly, brutally, lethally, by the Islamic State against Jews and Christians, and, yes, Muslims whom they disagree with.

It is a very sobering time. And so, quite rightly, our President, a week ago in his remarks, called upon the Congress to help him do something. The President gave his strategy. I listened with open ears to the President's strategy, and it was very curious to me because the President of the United States developed a strategy that consists of items that the United States is already doing. There was nothing new here.

The President called for an increase of 475 advisers to go into Iraq. The President said there wouldn't be any boots on the ground, of soldiers' boots.

He did not say that we are at war. Even though the Islamic State has declared war against the United States, the President did not say that the United States was going to war.

In fact, Mr. Speaker, something like 7 weeks ago, in the midst of the rise of the Islamic State in Iraq, with the horrific, breathtaking advances and murders, the President of the United States said that he wanted the Congress to withdraw the AUMF, which is the authorization of military force for the United States to be in Iraq.

It was really an unthinkable, bizarre request that this Congress received from the President. Would you please withdraw, the President said, my ability to be able to bring about military force in Iraq?

From my perspective, either the President and his advisers were incredibly shortsighted about this breathtaking rise of the Islamic State which, by the way, didn't just occur in the last 3 or 4 months. I am privileged to serve on the Intelligence Committee in the House of Representatives. We have watched, Mr. Speaker, literally, for the last several years, the rise of the Islamic State. We saw this coming.

That information presumably was available to the President of the United States as well. He knew they were on the rise. There has always been the Islamic jihad in the Middle East, but it has been at a different tempo. It has been on the rise.

Baghdadi, who is in his early to mid-forties, who is a very well-educated man with a doctorate degree, who literally has decades of veteran senior-level experience in al Qaeda, declaring war against the United States, literally, for decades, put himself in the position of being the top man at the very top of the hierarchy, the top of the line of the chain of command of the Islamic State. Baghdadi knew what he needed to have. He needed to be financially self-sustaining. To do that, he ordered the robbing of banks, particularly beginning in northern Iraq. Some reports estimate that the

Islamic State had stolen as much as over $400 million. We don't know the exact amount, but we do know that Baghdadi was determined, and he intended to advance. He knew he couldn't feed an army unless he had money to do so, and so he robbed it from the banks to begin his army.

Then he began to build that army by opening up prison doors and having prison breaks and bringing terrorists who had been jailed out of the prisons to join his band. So he had an army of terrorists, and he trained them even further, and he paid them with money that he stole from banks.

Then Baghdadi did something very strategic. He decided to steal oil fields, and he stole those oil fields in northern Iraq, very productive oil fields. One estimate says that one of the oil fields is worth about 10 billion barrels of oil. Whether or not that is true, that is one of the accounts that I have read. If that is true, it would be equal to about the value of the Bakken oil field, which has proven to be extremely productive and very lucrative in North Dakota here in the United States. Baghdadi is selling oil on the black market today to finance his terrorism, oil fields that he stole from northern Iraq and in the Kurdistan area.

He didn't stop there. He knew, to be viable, he also had to have refined energy products. So what did he do?

Baghdadi then stole and secured an oil refinery so that he could have oil products in order to have energy to run his army and also to be able to provide for the people under his protectorate. A ``protectorate'' is a very generous way of saying ``dictatorship'' in his caliphate. You see, he is the head guy. He is the caliph in his new self-described Islamic State, the caliphate.

You see, Mr. Speaker, he figured out how to finance himself. He took over electrical grids in Iraq and in Syria so that he could be the one who supplies the electricity to the people so that the people would be beholden to him. He put his people in charge of roads and supply lines. Baghdadi also took over a gas field in central Syria. That gas field also could be used to sell the gas for productivity or to deny that gas to Assad or to anyone he considered his enemy. You see, Baghdadi was strategic.

In August, I had the ability and the privilege to go over and visit both Turkey and Jordan and to meet with leadership there on the issue of ISIS, and, while I was there, it was stunning. There was a public display in Jordan of well over 15,000 who were protesting against Israel and in favor of the Muslim Brotherhood and the foreign terrorist-designated organization known as Hamas. There was also a reported demonstration of 7,000 Jordanians who were protesting in favor of the Islamic State. So there is pressure on Jordan--pressure within and pressure from without.

The Islamic State now controls checkpoints, so much so that there is, effectively, no longer a border between Iraq and Syria. That has been erased. Now Iraq and Syria have been joined to one another under the control and the authority of the Islamic State. They control checkpoints not only on Lebanon but also Israel.

It was horrifying to read that the Islamic State had joined up with the Free Syrian Army, the army that the United States has been involved with in the so-called ``vetting'' of moderates and in the training and equipping to fight against the Islamic State.

The Free Syrian Army reports say they had actually joined up with other Islamic jihadists, known as the Jabhat al-Nusra Front, and they took over the checkpoint that controls the area of the Golan Heights leading into Israel. There were upwards of 20 to 40 different U.N. peacekeepers at that checkpoint, and that checkpoint was taken over 200 yards from Israel, as if Israel didn't have enough to deal with in the terrorist organization known as Hezbollah, which is an Iranian proxy on her north, and from Russian influence as well coming through Hezbollah. Israel has had to suffer with indignities from Assad, from Syria, as well as from the Muslim Brotherhood franchise known as Hamas in Gaza.

It has been an extremely difficult summer. I met with refugees while I was in the Middle East region, people who were just peaceful, freedom-loving people just wanting to live their lives and raise their families and love people and worship their god. They were uprooted over this summer and late spring by Islamic jihad, both in Iraq. As for one woman I spoke to, she and her family were uprooted from their home in Iraq. They had to flee their home and abandon everything they owned and flee to Syria. Once they were in Syria, there was a rise of the Islamic jihad in Syria. They had to flee Syria and make their way to Turkey. When I spoke with her, she was on the southern border of Turkey, and she was hoping that she would have the ability, with her family, to move to the United States of America. She was going to go for yet one more final interview at the end of September, and she was hoping that her family would have that chance to come and live in freedom.

That is our wish, Mr. Speaker, for all men. We want all men to have the dignity of living in peace. It is why we honor the American Constitution today on Constitution Day. You see, this Constitution and this country mean something for the rest of the world. We think that the norms and the peacefulness that we enjoy and the prosperity that you see here in the United States must be somewhat normative across the world. We think, well, we have it, really, probably the best, but sometimes we don't recognize, really, how great we do have it. It isn't by accident--it is by design--and it came at a great cost and at a great sacrifice because our Founders recognized these ideals:

Number one, that all men are created equal and that we are endowed by our Creator with certain unalienable rights, rights that aren't given by government, rights that are only given by God: the right to life, to our liberty--our freedom--and to the pursuit of happiness, which means we have the privilege to work, and, once we work, we get to keep the fruit of our own labors.

What a brilliant concept. Where across the world do people have the right to life? Certainly not in Iraq today. Certainly not in Syria today. They don't enjoy the unfettered access to their right to life, because their life is imperiled by the Islamic State, which says to them: Under pain of death, you convert to Islam, or we kill you. You convert to Islam, or you pay us a tax. You convert to Islam, or you have to abandon everything you know and get as far away from us as you possibly can in the short term because we are coming after you in the long term.

Is that life? That is no life at all. But here in the United States, our Founders wisely understood that all of humanity's happiness springs from the right to life.

Number two, liberty, freedom. That is the hallmark and the emblem of the United States of America. If there is any ideal and any value, Mr. Speaker, that our Constitution champions it is this: it is liberty--freedom-- from an oppressive government that would force its will on an individual human's life, because the Holy Scriptures teach that life is precious. We are but a flower that quickly fades. We are but a puff of smoke, the Old Testament teaches in the Proverbs. Therefore, this life that God has given to us, that He has breathed into every human being, as He created every human being in His image and His likeness, this is it. This is no dress rehearsal. This is the main event.

Our Founders wisely understood that it is for freedom that we have been set free so that we can then aspire to do whatever it is that we choose to do, the way that we take our finger and write the poetry of each of our lives.

Then, in the Declaration of Independence, our Founders rightly said, through the pen of Thomas Jefferson's, that we are also endowed by our Creator--again, not by a government, not by any government. Only a God who created us, gave us the unalienable right to pursue happiness, which means we can pursue whatever employment, whatever labor that we so desire, and then we have the right, the unfettered right, to keep the fruit of our labor--to build a home, to marry, to start a family, to be able to go out and further and help our community. Oh, what a Nation we have today, Mr. Speaker, the economic powerhouse of the world, the military engine of the world. This is such a great and wonderful gift that was given to us.

That is why it is right and fitting and proper for us to honor and recognize this Constitution Day. I am so grateful and so honored and privileged that we can do exactly that and honor that day. That is why we have to stand for this liberty, something that people in other countries cannot do.

We must therefore observe, and it is why we have to make sure, when there is a great totalitarianism like the Islamic State, which has declared war against the United States, we have a decision to make. Anyone can declare war on you. It is another thing to bring about warlike acts against you in an attempt to defeat you. That is exactly what the Islamic State has done. That is exactly what they have stated their intention is. I believe, if there is anything, Mr. Speaker, that history has taught us it is this: when a madman speaks, we should listen. Baghdadi, most certainly, is rational from his point of view, but his ideas are mad, and, even further, they are immoral and they are evil to deprive life, liberty, and happiness to people.

If I could just pause and ask the Speaker if there is a time limitation that we are looking at. How much time remains?

The SPEAKER pro tempore. The gentlewoman from Minnesota has 27 minutes remaining.

Mrs. BACHMANN. I appreciate that update.

Mr. Speaker, we look at the threats that the United States is looking at from the Islamic State: the fact that they have declared war against the United States; the fact that they have already killed intentionally, in a cruel and barbaric manner, American citizens; the fact that they are recruiting American citizens to come and join them in their evil deed; the fact that

American citizens have left the Islamic State as terrorists under the creed of the Islamic State. Their creed says that those who join the Islamic State abandon any allegiance to any other government, including the American Government. They then become part of the Islamic State, and their duty and allegiance is to the Islamic State. Once they leave the Islamic State and return to the United States, then they have the ability to come in and be terrorists in the United States. This is nonsensical to me.

You see, Mr. Speaker, earlier this summer, I asked the FBI for a classified briefing. I did so because my home State of Minnesota has a tragic, very unfortunate, nexus to terrorism. We have the distinction of having the only convicted terrorist of 9/11 being from the State of Minnesota. His name is Moussaoui.

We also have a high number of Minnesotans who left Minnesota and abandoned the United States to go and fight on behalf of another al Qaeda organization, known as al-Shabaab. That is an al Qaeda affiliate in Somalia. Well over 50 Minnesotans traveled to join al-Shabaab and fight in the cause of Islamic jihad.

We also had terrorist financing cases, which were successfully prosecuted in Minnesota. Two women were convicted of terrorist financing cases in the Minneapolis Federal district court. Two women were convicted of terrorist financing in Rochester, Minnesota, in Federal district court.

Then we had the Westgate shopping mall terror act in Kenya, and from the terrorists who were involved and claimed sponsorship of this horrific act of the shooting at the Westgate mall in Kenya, the report was that two Minnesotans were a part of that effort. Then we saw, although it hasn't been confirmed by our government, that the terrorists have named two Minnesotans.

Then we saw that very sophisticated recruitment videos were put forth to recruit individuals to come and join al Qaeda. When this occurred, three of them were featured from Minnesota. They were called the ``Minnesota martyrs,'' three young men. One was a Caucasian American. His name was Troy Kastigar. He had been converted to Islam at a mosque called the Al Farooq mosque in Bloomington, Minnesota, where many of the individuals who have gone to fight on behalf of the Islamic State made their religious home.

Troy Kastigar said that he was honored to be a traitor to America. That was a part of his conviction to the Islamic State. He turned on his country;

so, when I asked the FBI earlier this summer--and then, of course we have had, according to the FBI, at minimum, another 20 Minnesotans who have left Minnesota to join the Islamic State, including the first two Americans who were killed fighting on behalf of the Islamic State, both of whom were from the State of Minnesota.

Just as recently as several weeks ago, three young Somali American girls left Minnesota, abandoned their families, and joined the Islamic State. We have a very unfortunate nexus.

It is with that background, Mr. Speaker, that I asked the FBI if I could come in and sit with them and if they would answer my questions in a classified setting.

I wanted to know, number one, had Minnesotans left the United States and joined to fight with the Islamic State. Unfortunately, I was told there were two. It was classified information at the beginning of the summer. Now, tragically, it has been reported worldwide that the very first two Americans were Minnesotans who were fighting for the Islamic State.

I asked the question: If these terrorists choose not to blow themselves up as suicide bombers, or if they are not killed fighting on behalf of the Islamic State, and they choose to fly back to the United States or gain entry to the United States legally through some other means with a U.S.-held passport, would they be given entry into the United States?

Mr. Speaker, I have to tell you, I was completely floored when the FBI said to me, ``Well, yes, of course, these terrorists would be allowed to come into the United States."

I asked, ``Why? And how?" They told me, ``We track them, and we put their names on a watch list." It isn't perfect, but the FBI puts the names of Americans on a watch list. I asked, ``What happens when they are on a watch list?"

I was told that the Americans with a U.S. passport, who have relinquished U.S. citizenship and have joined the Islamic State, have become terrorists and fought on behalf of the Islamic State then were returning to the United States, would be asked additional questions at screening at an airport before they come into the United States.

Mr. Speaker, I am asked additional questions, sometimes, at the airport. How could this be possible?

I was told by the FBI that the terrorists then would be given entry, and they would be allowed to go, unmolested, to return to their life here in the

United States.

Mr. Speaker, I submit that is pure madness for us to do that. If there was one thing we should do, it is follow our Constitution, follow the way of all nations, which is to secure the safety and security and sovereignty of that Nation.

To do that, Mr. Speaker, we must take the passports of anyone who has joined up with the Islamic State and do everything that we can to prevent terrorists from reentering the United States.

These terrorists would have had battlefield experience, they would have had established relationships with a terror network, and they potentially may have a plan for terrorist activity in the United States. That should and must be done.

What we also must do--and I agree with the President of the United States--we must defeat this enemy. The Islamic State has declared war against the United States. I believe that we must declare war against the Islamic State, but that is not what President Obama proposed.

You see, President Obama, from his rhetoric, has essentially made clear that he believes that war is obsolete in the 21st century, but that isn't the view of the Islamic State. That isn't the view of the totalitarian regime that has declared war against the United States. War isn't obsolete for their mind; yet the President of the United States is not choosing to engage the United States in war.

It is this odd hybrid where the President wants to say that he is going to try to defeat the Islamic State; yet he is not willing to do what it takes to defeat the Islamic State.

Why do I say that? Because the United States military is the greatest military--Army, Navy, and Air Force--in the world. There is nothing that can even remotely compare to the United States military; yet our President stated--both last week in his address to the Nation, as well as today at MacDill Air Force Base in his remarks--that there will be no U.S. boots on the ground. There will not be a U.S. military presence.

He is willing to use the American Air Force to fly missions and have airstrikes, but not boots on the ground.

You see, it doesn't work that way, Mr. Speaker. A military is a cohesive unit, and this is going up 50,000 feet, we have to understand: Do we have a problem? Yes, we have a problem.

Americans are being killed and beheaded by the Islamic jihadist state.

They have declared war against the United States. They are using all possible means to advance themselves to their goal.

They are gaining in strength every day--huge swaths of economic territory, huge swaths of geographic territory. They are increasing the size of their armies. They are making threats against the United States.

What is our response? The President of the United States, number one, is unwilling to declare war against this enemy. He is unwilling to use our United States military to defeat this enemy.

He has asked partners across the world--whether it is Muslim, Arab nations, whether it is our traditional allies--to join him. He received some rhetoric, some nods of the head, that some allies would help him; yet there isn't one word that one country is actually going to supply troops or supply armament or supply training.

We don't know what it is that the President has put together; yet, somehow, some way, he believes that this enemy is going to be defeated. His plan is what he was doing before. It was some advisers in an Embassy in Baghdad, U.S. advisers, but not boots on the ground.

His other avenue of defeat is to have United States tax dollars vet Syrians and, supposedly, Iraqis and train them to be a part of a military effort and give them American armament after 3 and a half weeks of arming.

You see, I really don't understand this methodology, when we already have the best military in the world and the President has decided to put the best option that we have on the sidelines and then he wants to create an ad hoc army on the ground with, at best, thin loyalties to our ultimate objective.

How thin, Mr. Speaker? Well, the RAND Corporation took a look at those who were trained, vetted, and on the ground and fighting in the Free Syrian Army, and the RAND Corporation found that about half--50 percent of those that the United States had vetted, the so-called moderates trained and given American armaments to--about half had been not only sympathetic but had cooperated and joined up with the enemy, the Islamic State and the al-Nusra front.

Well, if, in fact, the RAND Corporation is accurate and we have lost about 50 percent of those that we trained, I would say we don't have a very good success ratio.

As a matter of fact, what I would say is that the Islamic State has an incredible success ratio because we will have--at taxpayer expense-- identified, vetted, trained, and armed a whole new level of army for the

Islamic State, the enemy.

Who is this working for? Not us. Who is this defeating? Not them. Because the Islamic State continues to grow and we are paying for part of their military training and armaments.

In fact, this same story that came out last week said that the Islamic State had raided our United States weapons depots that we had set up for arming the Free Syrian Army.

What does the President want us to do? The President wanted the United States Congress to get behind his effort to increase the amount of training and arming of the Islamic State.

You see, these moderates have been more than a mirage, more than a charade for quite a bit of time. As a matter of fact, one of my colleagues from Minnesota gave me an article today before we took the vote.

Again, I am not trouncing anyone's vote in this chamber. I want to make it very clear. Both sides of the aisle--Republican and Democrat, individual Members of Congress--wrestled with their vote. Everyone struggled with what to do. Should we back the President in what he is choosing to do? Should we not back the President?

I give all goodwill to every Member of Congress. I castigate no one for the vote that they cast today because this was truly a vote of conscience that every Member made, and every Member needs to speak for themselves.

I only speak for myself tonight, Mr. Speaker, but this came out yesterday. The leader of the Free Syrian Army, the army that the President wants us to spend $500 million to train even more individuals, under this commander, this is what the article says: ``The Free Syrian Army announced they will not sign up to the U.S.-led coalition to destroy the Islamic State militants in Iraq and Syria."

I just want to repeat that again.

``The Free Syrian Army announced it will not sign up to the U.S.-led coalition to destroy ISIS in Iraq and Syria. The group's founder, Colonel Riad al-Asaad, stressed that toppling Syrian President Bashar al-Assad is their priority and that they will not join forces that U.S.-led efforts without a guarantee that the United States is committed to his overthrow.

`` `If they want to see the Free Syrian Army on their side' "--our side--`` `they should give assurances on toppling the Assad regime and on a plan including revolutionary principles.' "

This is the army that we are entrusting to win this effort against ISIS, and this army is more interested in toppling Assad. They are not interested in toppling ISIS.

``The announcement appears to be reversing an earlier statement on Thursday by the National Coalition opposition, the Free Syrian Army's political wing, which said it was ready to work with the coalition against IS."

The political arm said yes, but the guys who are actually going to have the boots on the ground say, ``No, we are not going to be there. We are not going to be fighting IS."

``Saying they had `long called for this action,' the coalition called on U.S. politicians to authorize the training and equipping of the Free Syrian Army `as soon as possible.' "

This is from the Middle East Eye. This is in an article that came out yesterday.

At best, we have got a very, very weak case--a very weak case. There are articles, which I agree with, that put the choice before us. It says: Do we have an enemy? Yes. What do we need to do? Defeat the enemy. I get that, but we have been unwilling to declare a war against this enemy. We have been unwilling to put the United States' military against this enemy.

What the President of the United States wants the United States to do is train some Syrians for 3 and a half weeks. We have already spent how many billion training the Iraqis, and the Iraqi Army could not stand up against the Islamic State army.

We had trained them for a very extensive period of time, with the finest training that we possibly could. They were well-equipped. Because United States residual forces were pulled by the President of the United States, the Iraqi Army could not stand up against the Islamic State, and they ran.

We think that 3 and a half weeks of training is going to do the job of the Syrians? I don't think so.

I think what the President of the United States asked us to do, Mr. Speaker, is to be a scapegoat in his failed strategy. He wants to be able to point to the Congress and say, ``The Congress gave me the authority to do it."

I don't want to do that. I didn't do that today. I chose to vote ``no." I am not being self-righteous when I say that.

My thinking on this is that I am willing to vote for a World War II strategy, meaning I am all in. I believe that we need to declare war against this evil empire of the Islamic State. We need to put all resources with the full plan, with an exit strategy in fully defeating the Islamic State, which we can. They are an army of 12,000.

This can be done, but I won't agree to a Vietnam war style strategy which is exactly, in my opinion, what President Obama chooses--chose to engage, with dribs and drabs, increasing a little here, increasing a little there.

The President, in my opinion, Mr. Speaker, would have been well-served if he also would have demonstrated even more humbleness regarding our strategy--meaning, for the President to be absolutely adamant last night, as well as today, for Secretary of State Kerry to be absolutely adamant today that there will be no U.S. boots on the ground sends a signal. It sends a signal that we are not serious about defeating this evil known as the Islamic State, which we must be.

I ask the question, Mr. Speaker: Who on the ground will be calling for the airstrikes against the Islamic State? Someone on the ground needs to do it. That is how war works. Someone who is on the ground needs to call for those airstrikes.

You cannot win a war when you only have overhead architecture and overhead surveillance. You need people on the ground who can go and gather the intelligence that you need so you know, effectively, how to defeat this enemy.

I ask this: Do we want to defeat this enemy decisively, quickly, and completely so that this enemy understands that, if they ever rear their head again, they had better think twice because we are going to so decimate their evil plan? Are we going to do that? Or are we going to do what happened in Vietnam, drib, drab, a little here, a little there, never quite getting up what it takes to actually defeat that enemy?

What happened in the end in Vietnam? Ultimately, the Communists came in, and that country fell. It was a very sad conclusion because, you see, the postscript to the story of Vietnam was the slaughter of innocents under the evil Pol Pot and the killing fields, and we know the history was an ugly history.

This isn't good, this is awful, but we need to see what has happened. You see, this Arab Spring has been nothing but Islamic bloodletting across the Middle East. In their own words, it is religious-based. In their own words, it is religious, shari'a inspired. In their own words, they are doing the bidding of their god to spill the blood of the infidel. This is an evil, this is a moral wrong, and this must be defeated.

The good news is it can be. We can defeat it. When we are the greatest military powerhouse in the world, when we have the capability to defeat this enemy, I don't understand it. I don't understand, Mr. Speaker, our President who just this week said that he needed to commit 3,000 American troops to the African continent for Ebola--to defeat Ebola.

Now, Ebola is a virus that has a health impact against the American people. I can understand dispatching medical personnel. I can understand dispatching people for humanitarian purposes, but the very weird thing about the President's strategy is it has been changing our military so that its purpose is to bring about humanitarian relief in the form of dispatching them for boots on the ground to deal with Ebola. That is not the purpose of a military.

The President needs to dispatch 3,000 troops--or whatever it takes--into the Islamic State to defeat the Islamic State. We don't go in willy-nilly. We go in with a very good plan, with the most brilliant military minds--and we have them--with the bravest military heroes--and we have them--and with the greatest military equipment that has ever been devised by man, and we have it. We have got it all. We have got the means for defeating this evil enemy.

To not do it, Mr. Speaker, in my mind, that is a moral wrong. That is an evil. To allow that evil to grow, thrive, and continue to slit the throats of men, women, and children; to rob them of their lives; and, yes, to see tragedy borne potentially across this land because, even today, as we are in this Chamber tonight, absolutely nothing has been done to secure America's southern border, absolutely nothing against entry by the Islamic State into this country, despite the fact that the Islamic State, through their social media, has been declaring their intent to do exactly that.

Why in the world aren't we closing our southern border and every other border and every other port of entry? Why aren't we pulling the passports of Americans who have become terrorists under the Islamic State and who seek to return to the United States?

Why would any sane country choose to take effective, commonsense answers to secure the safety of the American people? That is what a nation that wants to survive would do. That is the better way. That is what I hope the President of the United States will do because, you see, everything is at stake On this, our Constitution Day, let us recognize the first duty of any nation, especially the greatest Nation, is to secure the safety, sovereignty, and security of the American people. That, we must do, and I am so proud that we have the means to do it.

I believe that we will acquire the judgment to do what needs to be done. It is within the hearts of the American people. It is within our military. Now, it is up to the politicians. Listen to wisdom. Listen to the people, and do what needs to be done.

With that, Mr. Speaker, I yield back the balance of my time.

References

Hassan, Hassan (11 June 2014). "Political reform in Iraq will stem the rise of Islamists". The National. Retrieved 18 June 2014.

Khatib, Lina (12 June 2014). "What the Takeover of Mosul Means for ISIS". Carnegie Endowment for International Peace. Retrieved 18 June 2014.

"ISIS on offense in Iraq". Al-Monitor. 10 June 2014. Retrieved 11 June 2014.

Kelley, Michael B. (20 August 2014). "One Big Question Surrounds The Murder Of US Journalist James Foley By ISIS". Business Insider. Retrieved 20 August 2014. "...the de facto ISIS capital of Raqqa, Syria..."

^a b c d e f g Withnall, Adam (29 June 2014). "Iraq crisis: Isis changes name and declares its territories a new Islamic state with 'restoration of caliphate' in Middle East". The Independent. Retrieved 29 June 2014.

Rubin, Alissa J. (5 July 2014). "Militant Leader in Rare Appearance in Iraq". The New York Times. Retrieved 6 July 2014.

"ISIS Spokesman Declares Caliphate, Rebrands Group as Islamic State". SITE Institute. 29 June 2014. Retrieved 29 June 2014.

"Iraqi City in Hands of Al-Qaida-Linked Militants". Voice of America. 4 January 2014. Retrieved 16 January 2014.

"The Crisis in Iraq". UMAA. 18 June 2014. Retrieved 29 August 2014.

^a b c d Uppsala Data Conflict Programme: Conflict Encyclopaedia (Iraq). (See One-sided violence – ISIS-civilians – Actor information-ISIS.) Retrieved 5 August 2014.

"Al-Qaeda chief disbands main jihadist faction in Syria: Al-Jazeera". Hürriyet Daily News. 8 November 2013. Retrieved 12 July 2014.

^a b Knights, Michael (29 May 2014). "The ISIL's Stand in the Ramadi-Falluja Corridor". Combating Terrorism Center. Retrieved 12 July 2014.

"You Can't Understand ISIS If You Don't Know the History of Wahhabism in Saudi Arabia". August 28, 2014. Retrieved 2014-09-23.

Akhmeteli, Nina (9 July 2014). "The Georgian roots of Isis commander Omar al-Shishani". BBC News. Retrieved 9 July 2014.

^a b "Syria crisis: Omar Shishani, Chechen jihadist leader". BBC News. 3 December 2013. Retrieved 8 December 2013.

"Here's What We Know About the 'Caliph' of the New Islamic State". Business Insider. Agence France-Presse. 29 June 2014. Retrieved 18 July 2014.

Mohammed Tawfeeq and Laura Smith-Spark (4 January 2014). "Islamist group ISIS claims deadly Lebanon blast, promises more violence". CNN. Retrieved 22 January 2014.

"ISIS claims responsibility for Beirut car bomb". The Daily Star. 4 January 2014. Retrieved 22 January 2014.

^a b "Islamic State 'has 50,000 fighters in Syria'". Al Jazeera. 19 August 2014. Retrieved 19 August 2014.

ISIS has 100,000 fighters, growing fast - Iraqi govt adviser

^a b "IS has 20,000-31,500 fighters in Iraq and Syria: CIA". Yahoo! News. 12 September 2014. Retrieved 12 September 2014.

^a b Pool, Jeffrey (16 December 2004). "Zarqawi's Pledge of Allegiance to Al-Qaeda: From Mu'Asker Al-Battar, Issue 21". Terrorism Monitor 2 (24): The Jamestown Foundation. Archived from the original on 30 September 2007. Retrieved 30 July 2014.

"Al-Qaeda disavows ISIS militants in Syria". BBC News. 3 February 2014. Retrieved 3 February 2014.

^a b c d e "Philippines condemns, vows to 'thwart' ISIS". Rappler. 17 September 2014. Retrieved 19 September 2014.

^a b "Boko Haram voices support for ISIS' Baghdadi". Al Arabiya. 13 July 2014. Retrieved 24 August 2014.

"Al-Qaeda in Islamic Maghreb backs ISIS – Al-Monitor: the Pulse of the Middle East". Al-Monitor. Retrieved 23 August 2014.

Bill O'Reilly (1 October 2006). "Al-Qaeda in Yemen Declares Support for ISIS – Fox Nation". Fox News Channel. Retrieved 23 August 2014.

"BIFF, Abu Sayyaf pledge allegiance to Islamic State jihadists | GMA News Online". Gmanetwork.com. 16 August 2014. Retrieved 22 August 2014.

Dean, Sarah (21 August 2014). "PM Tony Abbott warns Australians of threats from Indonesian Jemaah Islamiyah group". Daily Mail. Retrieved 23 August 2014.

http://www.huffingtonpost.com/mohamed-elmenshawy/egypts-emerging-libya-pol_b_5703191.html

http://magharebia.com/en_GB/articles/awi/features/2014/07/31/feature-01

http://allafrica.com/stories/201407090299.html

http://www.al-monitor.com/pulse/security/2014/07/syria-iraq-isis-islamic-caliphate-global-recognition.html#

http://www.al-monitor.com/pulse/tr/originals/2014/02/isis-gaza-salafist-jihadist-qaeda-hamas.html

http://www.el-balad.com/1024731

Chikhi, Lamine (14 September 2014). "Splinter group breaks from al Qaeda in North Africa". Reuters. Retrieved 24 September 2014.

http://time.com/3273185/isis-us-nato/

^a b c d e f g h i j Helene Cooper (5 September 2014). "Obama Enlists 9 Allies". The New York Times. Retrieved 6 September 2014.

^a b Patrick Wintour (5 September 2014). "U.S. Forms 'core coalition' to fight ISIS militants in Iraq". The Guardian. Retrieved 6 September 2014.

"До 2020 година 1.8 млрд. лв. ще бъдат вложени в армията (1.8 bln. lv will be invested in the military by 2020)" (in Bulgarian). Dir.bg. 20 September 2014. Retrieved 20 September 2014.

^a b "Britain ready to supply Kurds with arms". Reuters. Retrieved 2014-08-18.

"Hrvatska u borbi protiv islamista: Na zahtjev SAD-a šaljemo oružje za iračku vojsku". Jutarnji list (in Croatian). 21 August 2014. Retrieved 22 August 2014.

http://www.sta.si/en/vest.php?s=a&id=2052615

Besar Likmeta (27 August 2014). "Albania Starts Shifting Weapons to Iraqi Kurds". Balkan Insight.

^a b "ISIS-rebel clashes resume in Deir al-Zor". The Daily Star. 18 June 2014. Retrieved 20 June 2014.

Aymenn Jawad al-Tamimi (11 May 2014). "Key Updates on Iraq's Sunni Insurgent Groups". Brown Moses blog. Retrieved 26 May 2014.

Category: POLITICS (23 July 2014). "Baath in Iraq declares war on ISIS". English.shafaaq.com. Retrieved 20 August 2014.

Hassan, Hassan (17 June 2014). "More Than ISIS, Iraq's Sunni Insurgency". Carnegie Endowment for International Peace. Retrieved 20 June 2014.

Mahdi, Osama (13 June 2014). "Council of the rebels begin appointing conservative management control areas". Elaph. Retrieved 21 August 2014.

Dehghanpisheh, Babak (3 August 2014). "Iran's elite Guards fighting in Iraq to push back Islamic State". Reuters.

"Iran Rushes Elite Quds Force Unit To Iraq To Help Government Stop ISIS Advance". weaselzippers.us. 11 June 2014. Retrieved 18 June 2014.

"In Pictures: Tension in Kirkuk". al Jazeera. Retrieved 18 July 2014.

"Jordan confirms its planes joined strikes on IS in Syria". Jordan Times. Retrieved 23 September 2014.

Ahmed, Raman (8 July 2014). "ISIL struggles for control over Syrian Kurdish areas". ARA News. Retrieved 9 July 2014.

"Presence of the MFS at the border of Iraq". Syriac International News Agency. 16 June 2014. Retrieved 30 July 2014.

Steinbach, Peter. "Die Christen in Syrien ziehen in die Schlacht". Die Welt. Retrieved 2 September 2014.

"The first detachment of the sons of our people from the Assyrian National Party fighters on the battlefield in the Nineveh Plain". Assyrian Patriotic Party. Retrieved 2 September 2014.

http://www.aina.org/news/20140810150643.htm

"مسيحيو العراق يتطوعون في قوات الدفاع عن المناطق المسيحية." LBC. Retrieved 26 August 2014.

Motlagh, Jason (20 July 2014). "Iraqi Christians under threat yet again". Gulf News. The Washington Post. Retrieved 8 August 2014.

"Syria conflict: President Assad finally turns on Isis". The Independent.

Mulcaire, Jack (22 April 2014). "Aleppo: Syria's Stalingrad?". The National Interest. Retrieved 29 April 2014.

"Al-Qaeda-linked Isis under attack in northern Syria". BBC News. 4 January 2014. Retrieved 15 January 2014.

Muslim, Hana (13 May 2014). "Syria rebels struggle for control over ISIL-held Raqqa". ARA News. Retrieved 16 May 2014.

"Syria rebels unite and launch new revolt, against jihadists". AFP. 4 January 2014. Retrieved 28 April 2014.

Sciutto, Jim; Schoichet, Catherine E.; Starr, Barbara (8 August 2014). "Obama authorizes 'targeted airstrikes' in Iraq to counter militants". CNN. Retrieved 8 August 2014.

Majumdar, Dave (8 August 2014). "U.S. Navy Strikes ISIS Targets in Iraq". USNI News. Retrieved 8 August 2014.

"U.S. fighter jets hit ISIS artillery with laser-guided, 500-pound bombs in Iraq: Pentagon". National Post.

"Air Force crews deliver 114,000 meals, 35,000 gallons of water in Iraq". Navy Times.

"Islamic State seizes territory inside Lebanon". The Telegraph. 4 August 2014.

Mortada, Radwan (19 May 2014). "Hezbollah fighters and the "jihadis": Mad, drugged, homicidal, and hungry". Al Akhbar (Lebanon). Retrieved 9 June 2014.

"TSK, IŞİD konvoyunu vurdu". Milliyet. Retrieved 1 February 2014.

"Türkiye IŞİD konvoyunu vurdu". dw.de. Retrieved 1 February 2014.

"TSK, Irak-Şam İslam Devleti Örgütü konvoyunu vurdu". CNN Turkey. Retrieved 1 February 2014.

"Turkish army returns fire from al-Qaeda-affiliated fighters on Syrian border". Today's Zaman. 16 October 2013. Retrieved 18 December 2013.

http://www.ntvmsnbc.com/id/25506321/

http://www.aksam.com.tr/guncel/istanbulda-isid-operasyonu/haber-294981

Spencer, Richard (3 July 2014). "Saudi Arabia sends 30,000 troops to Iraq border". The Telegraph. Retrieved 6 July 2014.

"Densus 88 tangkap aktivis ISIS dan ketua harian JAT". tribunnews.com. 11 August 2014. Retrieved 14 August 2014.

"Najib: Malaysia strongly condemns Islamic State militants". The Star. 28 August 2014. Retrieved 20 September 2014.

"Former Guantanamo detainee killed while leading jihadist group in Syria". The Long War Journal. 4 April 2014. Retrieved 19 May 2014.

"En Syrie, les Kurdes infligent une cuisante défaite aux jihadistes" [In Syria, the Kurds inflict a crushing defeat on the jihadists]. L'Orient-Le Jour. 18 July 2013. Archived from the original on 29 October 2013. Retrieved 18 July 2014.

Prothero, Mitchell (4 March 2014). "ISIS joins other rebels to thwart Syria regime push near Lebanon". The Sacramento Bee. McClatchy News. Retrieved 18 July 2014.

Ferran, Lee; Momtaz, Rym. "ISIS: Trail of Terror". ABC News. Retrieved 14 September 2014.

والبغدادي والشام العراق دون فقط"الإسلامية الدولة" وتسميتها الخلافة دولة تأسيس تعلن داعش" أميرها وتحذر لا عذر لمن يتخلف عن البيعة." Arabic CNN. 29 June 2014. Retrieved 31 July 2014 (Google translation available.).

"Isis rebels declare 'Islamic state' in Iraq and Syria". BBC News. 30 June 2014. Retrieved 30 June 2014.

"What is ISIS? — The Short Answer". The Wall Street Journal. 12 June 2014. Retrieved 15 June 2014.

"Security Council concerned about illicit oil trade as revenue for terrorists in Iraq, Syria". UN News Centre. 28 July 2014. Retrieved 17 August 2014.

Rieger, Sol (26 August 2014). "Israel Moves to Declare Support for ISIS Illegal as Photo of Groups Flag Appear". JP Updates. Retrieved 19 September 2014.

"Najib: Malaysia firmly against ISIS, organisation does no justice to Islam". Bernama. The Malay Mail. 6 September 2014. Retrieved 23 September 2014.

http://www.washingtonpost.com/blogs/worldviews/wp/2014/09/17/france-is-ditching-the-islamic-state-name-and-replacing-it-with-a-label-the-group-hates/

^a b c d e "The War between ISIS and al-Qaeda for Supremacy of the Global Jihadist Movement". Washington Institute for Near East Policy. June 2014. Retrieved 26 August 2014.

Ricks, Thomas E. (11 September 2006). "Situation Called Dire in West Iraq". The Washington Post. Retrieved 13 July 2014.

Linzer, Dafna; Ricks, Thomas E. (28 November 2006). "Anbar Picture Grows Clearer, and Bleaker". The Washington Post. Retrieved 18 July 2014.

Engel, Richard (27 December 2006). "Reporting under al-Qaida control". MSNBC. Retrieved 28 October 2009.

Engel, Richard (17 January 2007). "Dangers of the Baghdad plan". MSNBC. Archived from the original on 2 November 2007. Retrieved 28 October 2009.

"Iraqi neighbours rise up against al-Qa'eda". The Telegraph. 12 April 2008. Retrieved 27 August 2014.

Sly, Liz (23 July 2013). "Islamic law comes to rebel-held Syria". The Washington Post.

Lewis, Jessica (12 June 2014). "The Terrorist Army Marching on Baghdad". The Wall Street Journal. Retrieved 23 June 2014.(subscription required) Accessible via Google.

al-Salhy, Suadad (11 December 2013). "Al Qaeda tightens grip on western Iraq in bid for Islamic state". Reuters. Retrieved 23 June 2014.

^a b Sly, Liz (3 February 2014). "Al-Qaeda disavows any ties with radical Islamist ISIS group in Syria, Iraq". The Washington Post. Retrieved 7 February 2014.

McClam, Erin (20 June 2014). "More Extreme than al Qaeda? How ISIS compares to other terror groups". NBC News. Retrieved 28 June 2014.

Cockburn, Patrick (9 June 2014). "Battle to establish Islamic state across Iraq and Syria". The Independent. Retrieved 12 June 2014.

Whitlock, Craig (10 June 2006). "Death Could Shake Al-Qaeda In Iraq and Around the World". The Washington Post. Retrieved 22 July 2014.

^a b c "The Rump Islamic Emirate of Iraq". The Long War Journal. 16 October 2006. Retrieved 2 June 2014.

Fishman 2008, pp. 49–50.

^a b "ISI Confirms That Jabhat Al-Nusra Is Its Extension In Syria, Declares 'Islamic State Of Iraq And Al-Sham' As New Name of Merged Group". MEMRI. 8 April 2013. Retrieved 10 April 2013.

"Key Free Syria Army rebel 'killed by Islamist group'". BBC News. 12 July 2013.

"Al-Qaeda in Iraq confirms Syria's Nusra Front is part of its network". Al Arabiya. 9 April 2013. Retrieved 15 June 2014.

"Profile: Islamic State in Iraq and the Levant (ISIL)". BBC News. 11 June 2014. Retrieved 16 June 2014.

^a b Saxena, Vivek (18 June 2014). "ISIS vs ISIL – Which One Is It?". The Inquisitr. Retrieved 20 June 2014.

^a b Tharoor, Ishaan (18 June 2014). "ISIS or ISIL? The debate over what to call Iraq's terror group". The Washington Post. Retrieved 21 June 2014.

"Isis, Isil or Da'ish? What to call militants in Iraq". BBC News. 24 June 2014. Retrieved 16 August 2014.

^a b "Terrorist Designations of Groups Operating in Syria". United States Department of State. 14 May 2014. Retrieved 18 June 2014.

Abouzeid, Rania (16 January 2014). "Syria's uprising within an uprising". European Council on Foreign Relations. Archived from the original on 25 January 2014. Retrieved 15 August 2014.

Keating, Joshua (16 June 2014). "Who Is Abu Bakr al-Baghdadi?". Slate. Retrieved 22 July 2014.

Khosla, Simran (30 June 2014). "This Is What The World's Newest Islamic Caliphate Might Look Like". Business Insider (GlobalPost). Retrieved 22 July 2014.

"ISIL renames itself 'Islamic State' and declares Caliphate in captured territory". Euronews. 30 June 2014. Retrieved 30 June 2014.

"ISIS announces formation of Caliphate, rebrands as 'Islamic State'". The Long War Journal. 29 June 2014. Retrieved 30 June 2014.

Taylor, Adam (27 August 2014). "Meet 'QSIS': A new twist in what to call the extremist group rampaging in Iraq and Syria". The Washington Post.

Meky, Shounaz (24 August 2014). "Egypt's Dar al-Ifta: ISIS extremists not 'Islamic State'". Al Arabiya. Retrieved 27 August 2014.

Gambill, Gary (16 December 2004). "Abu Musab Al-Zarqawi: A Biographical Sketch". Terrorism Monitor 2 (24): The Jamestown Foundation. Archived from the original on 30 September 2007. Retrieved 30 July 2014.

"Zarqawi pledges allegiance to Osama". Dawn. Agence France-Presse. 18 October 2004. Archived from the original on 29 December 2007. Retrieved 13 July 2007.

"Al-Zarqawi group vows allegiance to bin Laden". NBC News. Associated Press. 18 October 2004. Retrieved 13 July 2007.

^a b "Al-Qaida in Iraq (AQI)". Dudley Knox Library. Naval Postgraduate School. Archived from the original on 1 April 2007. Retrieved 14 July 2014.

Whitaker, Brian (13 October 2005). "Revealed: Al-Qaida plan to seize control of Iraq". The Guardian. Retrieved 19 September 2014.

Fishman 2008, pp. 48–9.

"Al-Qaeda in Iraq names new head". BBC News. 12 June 2006.

Tran, Mark (1 May 2007). "Al-Qaida in Iraq leader believed dead". The Guardian.

^a b c d "Jihad Groups in Iraq Take an Oath of Allegiance". MEMRI. 17 October 2006. Retrieved 2 June 2014.

"al Qaeda's Grand Coalition in Anbar". The Long War Journal. 12 October 2006. Retrieved 2 June 2014.

^a b "Islamic State of Iraq Announces Establishment of the Cabinet of its First Islamic Administration in Video Issued Through al-Furqan Foundation". SITE Institute. 19 April 2007. Archived from the original on 28 September 2007. Retrieved 20 July 2014.

Phillips 2009, p. 74.

Mahnaimi, Uzi (13 May 2007). "Al-Qaeda planning militant Islamic state within Iraq". The Sunday Times (London). Archived from the original on 24 May 2011.

Targeting al Qaeda in Iraq's Network, The Weekly Standard, 13 November 2007

Ricks, Thomas; DeYoung, Karen (15 October 2007). "Al-Qaeda in Iraq Reported Crippled". The Washington Post.

Samuels, Lennox (20 May 2008). "Al Qaeda in Iraq Ramps Up Its Racketeering". Newsweek.(subscription required) Accessible via Google.

Phillips 2009, p. 65.

Kahl 2008.

Christie, Michael (18 November 2009). "Al Qaeda in Iraq becoming less foreign-US general". Reuters.

Arango, Tim (22 August 2014). "Top Qaeda Leaders in Iraq Reported Killed in Raid". The New York Times.

Shanker, Thom (4 June 2010). "Qaeda Leaders in Iraq Neutralized, US Says". The New York Times.

"US says 80% of al-Qaeda leaders in Iraq removed". BBC News. 4 June 2010.

"Attacks in Iraq down, Al-Qaeda arrests up: US general". Google News. Agence France-Presse. 4 June 2010.

Shadid, Anthony (16 May 2010). "Iraqi Insurgent Group Names New Leaders". The New York Times. Retrieved 22 August 2014.

"Abu Bakr al-Baghdadi: Islamic State's driving force". BBC World News. 31 July 2014. Retrieved 19 August 2014.

"U.S. Actions in Iraq Fueled Rise of a Rebel". The New York Times. 10 August 2014. Retrieved 28 August 2014.

"Military Skill and Terrorist Technique Fuel Success of ISIS". The New York Times. 27 August 2014. Retrieved 28 August 2014.

^a b "Al-Qaida: We're returning to old Iraq strongholds". Associated Press. 22 July 2012. Retrieved 22 August 2014.

^a b "Al Qaeda in Iraq Resurgent". Institute for the Study of War. September 2013. Retrieved 22 August 2014.

"Al Qaeda says it freed 500 inmates in Iraq jail-break". Reuters. 23 July 2013. Retrieved 22 August 2014.

Abouzeid, Rania (14 March 2014). "Syria: The story of the conflict". Politico. Retrieved 22 August 2014.

^a b Abouzeid, Rania (23 June 2014). "The Jihad Next Door". Politico. Retrieved 22 August 2014.

"Jabhat al-Nusra A Strategic Briefing". Quilliam Foundation. 8 January 2013. Retrieved 22 August 2014.

"Qaeda in Iraq confirms Syria's Nusra is part of network". GlobalPost. Agence France-Presse. 9 April 2013. Retrieved 9 April 2013.

"Al-Nusra Commits to al-Qaida, Deny Iraq Branch 'Merger'". Naharnet Agence France-Presse. 10 April 2013. Retrieved 18 May 2013.

Atassi, Basma (9 June 2013). "Qaeda chief annuls Syrian-Iraqi jihad merger". Al Jazeera. Retrieved 10 June 2013.

^a b "Iraqi al-Qaeda chief rejects Zawahiri orders". Al Jazeera. 15 June 2013. Retrieved 15 June 2013.

"Zawahiri disbands main Qaeda faction in Syria". The Daily Star. 8 November 2013. Retrieved 8 November 2013.

^a b c Birke, Sarah (27 December 2013). "How al-Qaeda Changed the Syrian War". New York Review of Books.

Vladimir Platov (18 January 2014). "Growth of International Terrorist Threat from Syria". New Eastern Outlook. Retrieved 11 June 2014.

"Chechen-led group swears allegiance to head of Islamic State of Iraq and Sham". The Long War Journal. 27 November 2013. Retrieved 13 July 2014.

Syrian branch of al Qaeda vows loyalty to Iraq's ISIS" France 24. 25 June 2014.

"Al Nusra pledges allegiance to Isil". Gulf News. 25 June 2014. Retrieved 29 June 2014.

Saad, Hwaida; Gladstone, Rick (4 January 2014). "Qaeda-Linked Insurgents Clash With Other Rebels in Syria, as Schism Grows". The New York Times. Retrieved 16 January 2014.

Casey, Mary Joshua Haber (7 January 2014). "Rebel factions continue fight against ISIL in Northern Syria". Foreign Policy. Retrieved 7 January 2014.

Sherlock, Ruth (2014-01-20). "Syria's Assad accused of boosting al-Qaeda with secret oil deals". Telegraph. Retrieved 2014-08-23.

http://www.telegraph.co.uk/news/worldnews/middleeast/syria/10585391/Syrias-Assad-accused-of-boosting-al-Qaeda-with-secret-oil-deals.html

http://world.time.com/2014/01/27/syria-assad-geneva-al-qaeda/

http://www.channel4.com/news/is-assad-isis-rebel-forces-iraq-syria

http://www.theguardian.com/world/2014/jun/26/beware-game-shadows-syria

Daragahi, Borzou; Jones, Sam; Kerr, Simeon (29 June 2014). "Iraq crisis: Isis declares establishment of a sovereign state". Financial Times. Retrieved 29 June 2014.(subscription required)

Zelin, Aaron Y. (30 June 2014). "ISIS Is Dead, Long Live the Islamic State". Foreign Policy (The Washington Institute). Retrieved 22 July 2014.

Cockburn, Patrick (30 June 2014). "Isis Caliphate has Baghdad worried because of appeal to angry young Sunnis". The Independent. Retrieved 2 July 2014.

"Iraq's Baghdadi calls for 'holy war'". Al Jazeera. 2 July 2014. Retrieved 2 July 2014.

Moore, Jack (2 July 2014). "Iraq Crisis: Senior Jordan Jihadist Slams Isis Caliphate". International Business Times UK. Retrieved 2 July 2014.

Mandhai, Shafik (7 July 2014). "Muslim leaders reject Baghdadi's caliphate". Al Jazeera. Retrieved 12 July 2014.

Goodenough, Patrick (6 July 2014). "Self-Appointed 'Caliph' Makes First Public Appearance". CNS News. Retrieved 26 July 2014.

Crilly, Rob; Mehsud, Saleem (9 July 2014). "Pakistani terror group swears allegiance to Islamic State". The Telegraph. Retrieved 13 August 2014.

Mekhennet, Souad (18 August 2014). "The terrorists fighting us now? We just finished training them.". The Washington Post.

"Syrians adjust to life under ISIS rule". The Daily Star. 29 August 2014. Retrieved 29 August 2014.

Fieldstadt, Elisha (29 June 2014). "ISIS Declare Themselves an Islamic State". NBC News. Retrieved 5 July 2014.

Gaouette, Nicole; Ajrash, Kadhim; Sabah, Zaid (23 June 2014). "Militants Seize Iraq-Jordan Border as Kerry Visits Baghdad". Bloomberg News. Retrieved 6 July 2014.

^a b Arango, Tim; Gordon, Michael R. (23 June 2014). "Iraqi Insurgents Secure Control of Border Posts". The New York Times. Retrieved 6 July 2014.

Abuqudairi, Areej (5 July 2014). "Anger boils over in the 'Fallujah of Jordan'". Al Jazeera. Retrieved 6 July 2014.

^a b Carey, Glen; Almashabi, Deema (16 June 2014). "Jihadi Recruitment in Riyadh Revives Saudi Arabia's Greatest Fear". Bloomberg News. Retrieved 17 June 2014.

^a b Solomon, Erika; Kerr, Simeon (3 July 2014). "Saudi Arabia sends 30,000 troops to Iraq border". Financial Times. Retrieved 6 July 2014. (subscription required)

Hall, Benjamin (23 June 2014). "ISIS joins forces with Saddam loyalists in bid to take Baghdad". Fox News Channel. Retrieved 31 August 2014.

"Boko Haram declares caliphate in Nigerian town under rebel control". Deutsche Welle. 24 August 2014. Retrieved 24 August 2014.

"Boko Haram Did Not Declare a Caliphate". Foundation for Defense of Democracies. 4 September 2014. Retrieved 12 September 2014.

"Nigeria military says one of its warplanes missing in northeast". Reuters. 14 September 2014. Retrieved 14 September 2014.

Arango, Tim (3 August 2014). "Sunni Extremists in Iraq Seize 3 Towns From Kurds and Threaten Major Dam". The New York Times. Retrieved 20 August 2014.

Smith-Spark, Laura (6 August 2014). "Iraqi Yazidi lawmaker: 'Hundreds of my people are being slaughtered'". CNN. Retrieved 20 August 2014.

"Statement by the President". The White House. 7 August 2014. Retrieved 18 August 2014.

Spencer, Richard (17 February 2014). "US-backed head of Free Syria Army voted out". The Telegraph.

Youseff, Nancy A. (26 May 2014). "Syrian Rebels Describe U.S.-Backed Training in Qatar". PBS. McClatchy News.

Masi, Alessandria (12 September 2014). "US-Backed Moderate Group In Syria Signs Truce With ISIS: Reports". International Business Times.

Akbar Shahid Ahmed; Ryan Grim (14 September 2014). "ISIS Strikes Deal With Moderate Syrian Rebels: Reports". The Huffington Post. Retrieved 21 September 2014.

"Foreign Terrorist Organizations". Bureau of Counterterrorism. United States Department of State. Retrieved 28 July 2014.

"Listed terrorist organisations". Australian National Security. Retrieved 31 July 2014.

"Currently listed entities". Public Safety Canada. Retrieved 31 July 2014.

http://www.resmigazete.gov.tr/eskiler/2013/10/20131010-1-1.pdf. Missing or empty |title= (help)

"Saudi Arabia designates Muslim Brotherhood terrorist group". Reuters. 7 March 2014. Retrieved 31 July 2014.

"Proscribed Terrorist Organisations". Home Office. 20 June 2014. Retrieved 31 July 2014.

"BNPT Declares ISIS a Terrorist Organization". Tempo. 2 August 2014. Retrieved 4 August 2014.

^a b Lister, Tim (13 June 2014). "ISIS: The first terror group to build an Islamic state?". CNN. Retrieved 14 June 2014.

^a b McCoy, Terrence (13 June 2013). "ISIS, beheadings and the success of horrifying violence". The Washington Post. Retrieved 23 June 2014.

Tran, Mark (11 June 2014). "Who are Isis? A terror group too extreme even for al-Qaida". The Guardian. Retrieved 11 June 2014.

Coughlin, Con; Whitehead, Tom (19 June 2014). "US should launch targeted military strikes on 'terrorist army' Isis, says General David Petraeus". The Telegraph. Retrieved 31 July 2014.

"Iraq religious leader supports liberation of Mosul, calls ISIS terrorists". Foreign Affairs Committee. National Council of Resistance of Iran. 13 June 2014. Retrieved 8 August 2014.

Uppsala Data Conflict Programme: Conflict Encyclopaedia (Iraq).(See War & minor conflict – Iraq: government – In depth – Continued armed conflict after USA's troop withdrawal from Iraq.) Retrieved 5 August 2014.

Beauchamp, Zack (20 June 2014). "The real roots of Iraq's Sunni-Shia conflict". Vox. Retrieved 27 June 2014.

^a b c Vick, Karl; Baker, Aryn (11 June 2014). "Extremists in Iraq Continue March Toward Baghdad". Time. Retrieved 23 June 2014.

Bilger, Alex (22 May 2014). "ISIS Annual Reports Reveal a Metrics-Driven Military Command". Institute for the Study of War. Retrieved 6 July 2014.

Cockburn, Patrick (15 June 2014). "Iraq crisis: West must take up Tehran's offer to block an Isis victory". The Independent. Retrieved 17 June 2014.

Mazzetti, Mark; Schmitt, Eric; Landler, Mark (10 September 2014). "Struggling to Gauge ISIS Threat, Even as U.S. Prepares to Act". The New York Times. Retrieved 11 September 2014.

Jeffrey Goldberg (10 August 2014). "Hillary Clinton: 'Failure' to Help Syrian Rebels Led to the Rise of ISIS". The Atlantic. Retrieved 10 August 2014.

The US, IS and the conspiracy theory sweeping Lebanon. BBC

'Password 360' Conspiracy Theories Linking CIA To Isis Actually Bring A Serious US Denial. The Huffington Post

Inside jobs and Israeli stooges: why is the Muslim world in thrall to conspiracy theories?. Mehdi Hassan. The New Statesman

Why Iran Believes the Militant Group ISIS Is an American Plot. Andy Baker. The New York Times. 19 July 2014

Holmes, Oliver (3 February 2014). "Al Qaeda breaks link with Syrian militant group ISIL". Reuters. Retrieved 6 July 2014.

^a b "Islamic State". Australian National Security. Australian Government. Retrieved 22 July 2014.

Hussain, Ghaffar (30 June 2014). "Iraq crisis: What does the Isis caliphate mean for global jihadism?". The Independent. Retrieved 6 July 2014.

Fernholz, Tim (1 July 2014). "Don't believe the people telling you to freak out over this "ISIL" map". Quartz. Retrieved 6 July 2014.

Paraszczuk, Joanna (7 February 2014). "Syria: Umar Shishani's Second-in-Command in ISIS Slams Scholars Who "Sow Discord" & Don't Fight". EA WorldView. Retrieved 8 July 2014.

"والبريطانية الأمريكية للمخابرات والعمالة بالتكفير ويتهمها(داعش) على يرد العرعور عدنان" المستشار (in arabic). Retrieved 8 July 2014.

:الأمريكيةسوريا للمخابرات والعمالة بالتكفير ويتهمها(داعش) على يرد العرعور عدنان" العهد".بالخوارج يصفهم و داعش من السوريين يحذر"العرعور" (in arabic). Retrieved 8 July 2014.

^a b "The slow backlash – Sunni religious authorities turn against Islamic State". The Economist. 6 September 2014.

Mamouri, Ali (29 July 2014). "Why Islamic State has no sympathy for Hamas". Al-Monitor. Retrieved 1 August 2014.

"Hamas appears in the Foreign Terrorist Organizations list of the US Department of State".

Zack Beauchamp (2 September 2014). "17 things about ISIS and Iraq you need to know". Vox Media. Retrieved 5 September 2014.

Abu Mohammad. "Letter dated 9 July 2005". Office of the Director of National Intelligence. Retrieved 22 July 2014. See page 2 onwards.

^a b c M. Alex Johnson (3 September 2014). "'Deviant and Pathological': What Do ISIS Extremists Really Want?". NBC News. Retrieved 5 September 2014.

Laith Kubba (7 July 2014). "Who is the U.S. targeting in Iraq air strikes?". Al Jazeera.

Tran, Mark; Weaver, Matthew (30 June 2014). "Isis announces Islamic caliphate in area straddling Iraq and Syria". The Guardian. Retrieved 6 July 2014.

McGrath, Timothy (2 July 2014). "Watch this English-speaking ISIS fighter explain how a 98-year-old colonial map created today's conflict". Los Angeles Times. GlobalPost. Retrieved 22 July 2014.

Romain Caillet (27 December 2013). "The Islamic State: Leaving al-Qaeda Behind". Carnegie Endowment for International Peace.

^a b "ISIS' 'Southern Division' praises foreign suicide bombers". The Long War Journal. 9 April 2014. Retrieved 2 June 2014.

"Middle East –وعراقية سورية أراض على"الفرات ولاية" قيام يعلن الإسلامية الدولة تنظيم– 24". France 24. 31 August 2014. Retrieved 6 September 2014. فرانس

Aymenn Jawad Al-Tamimi (10 September 2014). "Islamic State "Euphrates Province" Statement: Translation and Analysis". aymennjawad.org. Retrieved 20 September 2014.

Thompson, Nick; Shubert, Attika (18 September 2014). "The anatomy of ISIS: How the 'Islamic State' is run, from oil to beheadings". CNN. Retrieved 21 September 2014.

Ben Hubbard (24 July 2014). "Life in a Jihadist Capital: Order With a Darker Side". The New York Times. Retrieved 5 September 2014.

^a b Charles C. Caris; Samuel Reynolds (July 2014). "ISIS Governance in Syria". Institute for the Study of War.

Mariam Karouny (4 September 2014). "In northeast Syria, Islamic State builds a government". Reuters.

^a b Zelin, Aaron Y. (13 June 2014). "The Islamic State of Iraq and Syria Has a Consumer Protection Office". The Atlantic. Retrieved 17 June 2014.

Gardner, Frank (9 July 2014). "'Jihadistan': Can Isis militants rule seized territory?". BBC News. Retrieved 17 August 2014.

Richard Spencer (16 September 2014). "Islamic State issues new school curriculum in Iraq". The Telegraph.

"ISIS eradicates art, history and music from curriculum in Iraq". CBS News. 15 September 2014.

Zaid Sabah; Khalid Al-Ansary (17 September 2014). "Mosul Schools Go Back in Time With Islamic State Curriculum". Bloomberg News.

Catherine Philp (17 September 2014). "Parents boycott militants' curriculum". The Times.

^a b "Iraq: Isis warns women to wear full veil or face punishment". The Guardian. Reuters. Retrieved 27 July 2014.

"Islamic State says women in Mosul must wear full veil or be punished". The Irish Times. 26 July 2014. Retrieved 23 August 2014.

"Islamic State tells Mosul shopkeepers to cover up naked mannequins". Daily News.

Taylor, Adam (12 June 2014). "The rules in ISIS' new state: Amputations for stealing and women to stay indoors.". The Washington Post. Retrieved 2 August 2014.

"ISIS bans music, imposes veil in Raqqa". Al-Monitor. 20 January 2014. Retrieved 13 September 2014.

"Convert, pay tax, or die, Islamic State warns Christians". The Guardian. Reuters. 18 July 2014. Retrieved 27 July 2014.

Abedine, Saad; Mullen, Jethro (28 February 2014). "Islamists in Syrian city offer Christians safety – at a heavy price". CNN. Retrieved 27 July 2014.

Hubbard, Ben. "Life in a Jihadist Capital: Order With a Darker Side". The NewYork Times. Retrieved 27 July 2014.

Nebehay, Stephanie (8 September 2014). "New U.N. rights boss warns of 'house of blood' in Iraq, Syria". Reuters. Retrieved 9 September 2014.

"UN 'may include' Isis on Syrian war crimes list". BBC News. 26 July 2014

UN accuses Islamic State group of war crimes Al Jazeera 27 Aug 2014

"Syria conflict: Islamic State 'committed war crimes'". BBC News. 27 August 2014. Retrieved 2 September 2014.

Bulos, Nabih (20 June 2014). "Islamic State of Iraq and Syria aims to recruit Westerners with video". Los Angeles Times. Retrieved 17 August 2014.

Abi-Habib, Maria (26 June 2014). "Iraq's Christian Minority Feels Militant Threat". The Wall Street Journal. Retrieved 6 July 2014.(subscription required) Accessible via Google.

http://www.bbc.com/news/world-middle-east-29026491

"ISIL Militants Killed More Than 1000 Civilians In Recent Onslaught In recent Onslaught in Iraq: UN". RT News. Retrieved 4 July 2014.

"Iraq violence: UN confirms more than 2000 killed, injured since early June". UN News Centre. 24 June 2014. Retrieved 4 July 2014.

"UN warns of war crimes as ISIL allegedly executes 1,700". Today's Zaman. 15 June 2014. Retrieved 4 July 2014.

Spencer, Richard (16 June 2014). "Iraq crisis: UN condemns 'war crimes' as another town falls to Isis". The Telegraph. Retrieved 6 July 2014.

"Syria: ISIS Summarily Killed Civilians". Human Rights Watch. 14 June 2014. Retrieved 5 July 2014.

"Syria conflict: Amnesty says ISIS killed seven children in north". BBC News. 6 June 2014. Retrieved 5 July 2014.

"NGO: ISIS kills 102-year-old man, family in Syria". Al Arabiya. Retrieved 7 July 2014.

"Armed Children as Young as 9 Patrolling Streets of Mosul". The Clarion Project. 3 July 2014. Retrieved 9 July 2014.

"Surging Violence Against Women in Iraq". Inter Press Service. 27 June 2014. Retrieved 5 July 2014.

Winterton, Clare (25 June 2014). "Why We Must Act When Women in Iraq Document Rape". The Huffington Post. Retrieved 10 July 2014.

جهاد"لـ المتزوجات غير بتقديم الموصل أهالي يطالب"داعش" :كويتي إعلامي."علي محمد إسراء النكاح."اليوم المصرى. Retrieved 10 July 2014.

Susskind, Yifat (3 July 2014). "Under Isis, Iraqi women again face an old nightmare: violence and repression". The Guardian. Retrieved 17 July 2014.

"Hanaa Edwar". NGO Working Group on Women, Peace and Security. Retrieved 13 September 2014.

^a b Mike, Giglio (27 June 2014). "Fear Of Sexual Violence Simmers In Iraq As ISIS Advances". BuzzFeed. Retrieved 9 July 2014.

Ruth, Sherlock (26 June 2014). "Hague urges unity as Iraq launches first counter-attack". The Telegraph. Retrieved 9 July 2014.

Williams, Martin (25 September 2013). "Sexual jihad is a bit much". The Citizen. Retrieved 7 July 2014.

Brekke, Kira (8 September 2014). "ISIS Is Attacking Women, And Nobody Is Talking About It". The Huffington Post. Retrieved 11 September 2014.

Ahmed, Havidar (14 August 2014). "The Yezidi Exodus, Girls Raped by ISIS Jump to their Death on Mount Shingal". Rudaw Media Network. Retrieved 26 August 2014.

Stone, Jeff (17 June 2014). "ISIS Attacks Twitter Streams, Hacks Accounts To Make Jihadi Message Go Viral". International Business Times. Retrieved 19 June 2014.

"US targets al Qaeda's al Furqan media wing in Iraq". The Long War Journal. 28 October 2007. Retrieved 24 June 2014.

Bilger 2014, p. 1.

Zelin, Aaron Y. (8 March 2013). "New statement from the Global Islamic Media Front: Announcement on the Publishing of al-I'tiṣām Media Foundation – A Subsidiary of the Islamic State of Iraq – It Will Be Released Via GIMF". JIHADOLOGY. Retrieved 24 June 2014.

Gertz, Bill (13 June 2014). "New Al Qaeda Group Produces Recruitment Material for Americans, Westerners". The Washington Free Beacon. Retrieved 24 June 2014.

"ISIS Declares Islamic Caliphate, Appoints Abu Bakr Al-Baghdadi As 'Caliph', Declares All Muslims Must Pledge Allegiance To Him". MEMRI. 30 June 2014. Retrieved 7 July 2014.

"ISIL Launches 'Ajnad Media Foundation' to Specialize in Jihadi Chants". SITE Institute. 15 January 2014. Retrieved 25 June 2014.(subscription required)

"Dabiq: What Islamic State's New Magazine Tells Us about Their Strategic Direction, Recruitment Patterns and Guerrilla Doctrine". The Jamestown Foundation. 1 August 2014. Retrieved 18 August 2014.

"Dabiq: The Strategic Messaging of the Islamic State". Institute for the Study of War. 15 August 2014. Retrieved 18 August 2014.

^a b Roula Khalaf and Sam Jones (17 June 2014). "Selling terror: how Isis details its brutality". Financial Times. Retrieved 18 June 2014.

Berger, J. M. (16 June 2014). "How ISIS Games Twitter". The Atlantic. Retrieved 19 June 2014.

"ISIS Propaganda Campaign Threatens U.S.". Anti-Defamation League. 27 June 2014. Retrieved 27 June 2014.

Sheera, Frenkel (16 June 2014). "Meet The 'ISIS Fanboys' Spreading The Message Of Iraq's Most Feared Terror Group". BuzzFeed.

Dan Friedman (17 August 2014). "Twitter stepping up suspensions of ISIS-affiliated accounts: experts". Daily News. New York. Retrieved 8 September 2014.

"ISIS Faces Resistance From Social Media Companies". Anti-Defamation League. 23 July 2014. Retrieved 24 July 2014.

"Second US journalist held by ISIS at risk of being executed". Miami News. 23 August 2014. Retrieved 23 August 2014.

Jalabi, Raya (2 September 2014). "Video of Steven Sotloff beheading bears many similarities to James Foley killing". The Guardian. Retrieved 3 September 2014.

^a b "IS jihadi group beheads US journalist Steven Sotloff". CNN. 2 September 2014. Retrieved 17y September 2014.

"A Second Message to America". Al-Furqan Media Productions.

Holmes, Oliver (13 September 2014). "Islamic State video purports to show beheading of UK hostage David Haines". Reuters. Retrieved 13 September 2014.

^a b c d Allam, Hannah (23 June 2014). "Records show how Iraqi extremists withstood U.S. anti-terror efforts". McClatchy News. Retrieved 25 June 2014.

Chulov, Martin (15 June 2014). "How an arrest in Iraq revealed Isis's $2bn jihadist network". The Guardian. Retrieved 17 June 2014.

Moore, Jack (11 June 2014). "Mosul Seized: Jihadis Loot $429m from City's Central Bank to Make Isis World's Richest Terror Force". International Business Times UK. Retrieved 19 June 2014.

McCoy, Terrence (12 June 2014). "ISIS just stole $425 million, Iraqi governor says, and became the 'world's richest terrorist group'". The Washington Post. Retrieved 18 June 2014.

Carey, Glen; Haboush, Mahmoud; Viscusi, Gregory (26 June 2014). "Financing Jihad: Why ISIS Is a Lot Richer Than Al-Qaeda". Bloomberg News. Retrieved 19 July 2014.

"U.S. Official Doubts ISIS Mosul Bank Heist Windfall". NBC News. 24 June 2014. Retrieved 22 July 2014.

Daragahi, Borzou (17 July 2014). "Biggest bank robbery that 'never happened' – $400m Isis heist". Financial Times. Retrieved 21 July 2014.(subscription required) Accessible via Google.

Rogin, Josh (14 June 2014). "America's Allies Are Funding ISIS". The Daily Beast. Retrieved 19 June 2014.

"Iraq crisis: How Saudi Arabia helped Isis take over the north of the country". The Independent. 13 July 2014. Retrieved 9 August 2014.

Parker, Ned; Ireland, Louise (9 March 2014). "Iraqi PM Maliki says Saudi, Qatar openly funding violence in Anbar". Reuters.

"Maliki: Saudi and Qatar at war against Iraq". Al Jazeera. 9 March 2014.

"Maliki accuses Saudi Arabia of backing rebels". Al Arabiya. 17 June 2014. Retrieved 17 June 2014.

^a b Bozorgmehr, Najmeh; Kerr, Simeon (25 June 2014). "Iran-Saudi proxy war heats up as Isis entrenches in Iraq". Financial Times. Retrieved 29 June 2014.

Hauslohner, Abigail (13 June 2014). "Jihadist expansion in Iraq puts Persian Gulf states in a tight spot". The Washington Post. Retrieved 18 June 2014.

Black, Ian (19 June 2014). "Saudi Arabia rejects Iraqi accusations of Isis support". The Guardian. Retrieved 19 June 2014.

Chulov, Martin (15 June 2014). "Iraq arrest that exposed wealth and power of Isis jihadists". The Guardian. Retrieved 16 June 2014.

Solomon, Erika (28 April 2014). "Syria's jihadist groups fight for control of eastern oilfields". Financial Times. Retrieved 17 June 2014.

Fisher, Max (12 June 2014). "How ISIS is exploiting the economics of Syria's civil war". Vox. Retrieved 17 June 2014.

Matthews, Dylan (24 July 2014). "The surreal infographics ISIS is producing, translated". Vox. Retrieved 25 July 2014.

"Two Arab countries fall apart". The Economist (14 June 2014). Retrieved 18 July 2014.

"The Syrian rebel groups pulling in foreign fighters". BBC News. 24 December 2013. Retrieved 24 December 2013.

"Chechen fighter emerges as face of Iraq militant group". Fox News Channel. Associated Press. 2 July 2014.

Schmidt, Michael S. (15 September 2014). "U.S. Pushes Back Against Warnings That ISIS Plans to Enter From Mexico". The New York Times. Retrieved 16 September 2014.

"Insight Into How Insurgents Fought in Iraq". The New York Times. 17 October 2013. Retrieved 22 August 2014.

^a b "Not Just Iraq: The Islamic State Is Also on the March in Syria". The Huffington Post. 7 August 2014. Retrieved 11 August 2014.

^a b c Gibbons-Neff, Thomas (18 June 2014). "ISIS propaganda videos show their weapons, skills in Iraq". The Washington Post. Retrieved 11 August 2014.

"US-made Stinger missiles have likely fallen into ISIS hands, officials say". Fox News Channel. 16 June 2014. Retrieved 21 June 2014.

^a b c Jeremy Bender (9 July 2014). "As ISIS Routs The Iraqi Army, Here's A Look At What The Jihadists Have In Their Arsenal". Business Insider. Retrieved 11 August 2014.

Prothero, Mitchell (14 July 2014). "Iraqi army remains on defensive as extent of June debacle becomes clearer". Stars and Stripes. Retrieved 15 July 2014.

Chelsea J. Carter; Tom Cohen; Barbara Starr (9 August 2019). "U.S. jet fighters, drones strike ISIS fighters, convoys in Iraq". CNN. Retrieved 5 September 2014.

"ISIS Holds Parade With Captured US Military Vehicles". Zero Hedge. 25 June 2014. Retrieved 16 August 2014.

Tilghman, Andrew; Schogol, Jeff (12 June 2014). "How did 800 ISIS fighters rout 2 Iraqi divisions?". Military Times. Retrieved 14 June 2014.

"State of emergency: ISIS militants overrun Iraq city of 1.8mn, free 2,500 prisoners". RT News. 18 June 2014. Retrieved 22 July 2014.

"Isis leader calls on Muslims to 'build Islamic state'". BBC News. 1 July 2014. Retrieved 2 July 2014.

"Al Qaeda Militants Capture US Black Hawk Helicopters In Iraq". Zero Hedge. 10 June 2014. Retrieved 14 June 2014.

Lake, Eli; Dettmer, Jamie; De Visser, Nanette (11 June 2014). "Iraq's Terrorists Are Becoming a Full-Blown Army". The Daily Beast. Retrieved 15 July 2014.

Beaumont, Peter (12 June 2014). "How effective is ISIS compared with the Iraqi army and the Kurdish peshmerga?". The Guardian. Retrieved 14 June 2014.

Cowell, Alan (10 July 2014). "Low-Grade Nuclear Material Is Seized by Rebels in Iraq, U.N. Says". The New York Times. Retrieved 15 July 2014.

Sherlock, Ruth (10 July 2014). "Iraq jihadists seize 'nuclear material', says ambassador to UN". The Telegraph. Retrieved 15 July 2014.

Uppsala Data Conflict Programme: Conflict Encyclopaedia (Iraq).(See War & minor conflict – Iraq: government – In depth – 2004–2009 the Al-Qaida ally ISI and its predecessors TQJBR and MSC.) Retrieved 5 August 2014.

Peter Grier, Faye Bowers (8 June 2007). "Iraq's bin Laden? Zarqawi's rise". The Christian Science Monitor. Retrieved 13 July 2007.

Uppsala Data Conflict Programme: Conflict Encyclopaedia (Iraq).(See War & minor conflict – Iraq: government – Active dyads in this conflict – Iraq: government (entire conflict).) Retrieved 5 August 2014.

^a b Uppsala Data Conflict Programme: Conflict Encyclopaedia (Iraq).(See One-sided violence – ISIL-civilians.) Retrieved 5 August 2014.

Uppsala Data Conflict Programme: Conflict Encyclopaedia (Iraq). (See One-sided violence – ISIS-civilians – Actor information-Summary.) Retrieved 5 August 2014.

Parker, Ned (27 June 2007). "Christians forced out of Baghdad district". Los Angeles Times. Retrieved 27 June 2007.

"Iraqi ministry: Militant leader arrested in Baghdad". CNN. 10 March 2007. Archived from the original on 11 March 2007. Retrieved 14 July 2014.

"Captured Iraqi not al-Baghdadi". Al Jazeera. 10 March 2007. Archived from the original on 12 March 2007. Retrieved 19 July 2014.

Anjarini, Suhaib (2 July 2014). "Al-Baghdadi following in bin Laden's footsteps". Al Akhbar (Lebanon). Retrieved 20 July 2014.

^a b "Wanted: Abu Du'a – Up to $10 Million". Rewards for Justice Program. Retrieved 8 October 2011.

"Most wanted names of terror world". Hindustan Times. 3 April 2012. Retrieved 12 September 2013.

"Abdullah al Janabi openly preaches in Fallujah mosque". The Long War Journal. 18 January 2014. Retrieved 13 September 2014.

"Unconfirmed report: Abu Omar al Baghdadi killed; Al Qaeda's information minister confirmed killed". The Long War Journal. 3 May 2007. Retrieved 22 July 2014.

"U.S. says terrorist in Jill Carroll kidnapping killed". CNN. 4 May 2007. Retrieved 22 July 2014.

Marquez, Jeremiah (24 May 2007). "SoCal family mourns soldier found dead in Iraq river". U-T San Diego. Associated Press. Retrieved 16 November 2013.

Michael Zitz: "With men still missing, a soldier returns to Iraq". Free Lance-Star, 27 June 2007. Retrieved 27 June 2007.

"US launches major Iraq offensive". BBC News.19 June 2007. Retrieved 27 June 2007.

"Suicide bomber kills 13 at busy Baghdad hotel". The Washington Times. 26 June 2014. Retrieved 13 August 2013.

"Police Release Tribal Shaykhs' Names". IraqSlogger, 27 June 2007. Retrieved 27 June 2007.

Tran, Mark (26 June 2007). "Al-Qaida linked to Baghdad hotel bombing". The Guardian. Retrieved 19 July 2014.

"Brit Security Firm Faulted in Hotel Bombing". IraqSlogger, 27 June 2007. Retrieved 27 June 2007.

"Al Mansour Hotel, Baghdad". Yahoo! Travel, 5 February 2007. Retrieved 27 June 2007.

Drummond, Mike (27 June 2007). "Two tribal leaders killed in Baghdad". The Miami Herald. McClatchy News. Retrieved 27 June 2007

Cordover, Adam B (9 July 2007). "Al-Qaeda Issues Ultimatum to Iran". Cafe Cordover. Retrieved 19 July 2014.

Al-Mufti, Nermeen. "More death and political intrigue". Al-Ahram Weekly. 5–11 July 2007. Issue 852. Retrieved 30 July 2014..

"Baghdad bomb fatalities pass 150". BBC News. 26 October 2009. Retrieved 26 October 2009.

"Baghdad car bombs cause carnage". BBC News. 8 December 2009. Retrieved 8 December 2009.

"Qaeda in Iraq claims deadly central bank raid". Agence France-Presse. 17 June 2010. Archived from the original on 3 March 2014. Retrieved 12 September 2013.

al-Ansary, Khalid (20 August 2010). "Al Qaeda claims responsibility for attack in Iraq". Reuters.

"Hostages Killed in Al-Qaeda Attack on Baghdad Church". Al-Manar. Agence France-Presse. 1 November 2010. Retrieved 6 November 2010.

"Al-Qaeda claims Iraq church attack". Al Jazeera. 2 November 2010. Retrieved 6 November 2010.

"Al Qaeda in Iraq calls Egypt protesters to wage jihad". Dawn. Agence France-Presse. 9 February 2011. Retrieved 16 November 2013.

Nordland, Rod (25 July 2012). "Al Qaeda Taking Deadly New Role in Syria Conflict". The New York Times. Retrieved 25 July 2012.

Brett Barrouquere (16 August 2012). "Iraqis in Ky. linked to IED attack zone". Army Times. Associated Press. Retrieved 27 August 2012.

^a b Gul Tuysuz, Raja Razek, Nick Paton Walsh (6 November 2013). "Al Qaeda-linked group strengthens hold in northern Syria". CNN. Retrieved 3 December 2013.

"Death toll rises to 42 as explosions hit Turkish town on border with Syria". Hürriyet Daily News. 11 May 2013. Retrieved 11 May 2013.

"Deadliest Terror Attack in Turkey's History Might Be Another Attempt to Derail Peace Talks? But Which One? Syria or PKK?". The Istanbulian. 11 May 2013. Retrieved 11 May 2013.

Hacaoglu, Selcan; El Baltaji, Dana (12 May 2013). "Turkey Holds Nine Suspects in Deadly Attack Blamed on Syria". Bloomberg Businessweek. Retrieved 19 July 2014.

Dorell, Oren (12 May 2013). "Turkey: 9 with Syrian ties arrested in car bombings". USA Today. Retrieved 15 July 2014.

"Turkey charges prime suspect in car bombings, report says". Al Arabiya. 21 May 2013. Retrieved 18 June 2014.

Morris, Loveday; DeYoung, Karen (12 July 2013). "Al-Qaeda-affiliated gunmen kill Syrian rebel commander, rebels say". The Washington Post. Retrieved 3 July 2014.

^a b "Iraq:hundreds escape from Abu Ghraib jail". The Guardian. Associated Press. 22 July 2013. Retrieved 24 July 2013.

^a b Schreck (23 July 2013). "Abu Ghraib Prison Break: Al Qaeda in Iraq Claims Responsibility for Raid". The Huffington Post. Retrieved 24 July 2013.

Lake, Eli (29 July 2013). "Al Qaeda in Iraq Abu Ghraib Jailbreak a Counterterrorism Nightmare". The Daily Beast. Retrieved 1 August 2013.

Malas, Nour; Abushakra, Rima (6 August 2013). "Islamists Seize Airbase Near Aleppo". The Wall Street Journal. Retrieved 16 July 2014.(subscription required) Accessible via Google.

Luca, Ana Maria (11 November 2013). "Message from Ayman al-Zawahiri". NOW News. Retrieved 22 January 2014.

Loyd, Anthony (20 September 2013). "Will I die today? Face to face with jihadists fuelled by hate". The Australian. Retrieved 16 July 2014.(subscription required) Accessible via Google.

Burch, Jonathon; Dziadosz, Alexander (19 September 2013). "Syrian rebels, Qaeda group clash near Turkish border crossing". Reuters. Retrieved 16 July 2014.

Al-Qaeda group and FSA declare truce as Turkey keeps Syria border gate closed Hürriyet Daily News, 19 September 2013

Syrian al-Qaeda prepares to launch attack in Turkey's big cities Today's Zaman, 4 November 2013

"Reyhanlı saldırısını El Kaide üstlendi". Oda TV. 1 October 2013.

"Al-Qaeda Claims Responsibility for Reyhanlı". Aydınlık. 2 October 2013. Retrieved 21 January 2014.

"ISIL threatens Erdoğan with suicide bombings in Ankara, İstanbul". Today's Zaman. 30 September 2013. Retrieved 21 January 2014.

"El Kaide, Reyhanlı'yı üstlendi iddiası". CNN Türk. 1 October 2013.

Surk, Barbara (10 December 2013). "Syrian army pounds rebels near Lebanon border". Yahoo! News. Retrieved 18 December 2013.

Gathmann, Florian; Meiritz, Annett (1 September 2014). "Iraq debate in the Bundestag: Good weapons, evil weapons". Spiegel Online. Retrieved 1 September 2014.

Marszal, Andrew; Sanchez, Raf; Henderson, Barney (2 September 2014). "Steven Sotloff 'beheaded by Islamic State' – latest". The Telegraph. Retrieved 2 September 2014.

"After James Foley, ISIS beheads another US journalist Steven Sotloff". The Times of India. 3 September 2014. Retrieved 3 September 2014.

http://www.smh.com.au/world/islamic-state-says-vladimir-putins-throne-is-under-threat-and-will-fall-when-we-come-to-you-20140904-10c4hq.html#ixzz3CIY8T9SZ

Original video with English subtitles and transcript by MEMRI at Jim Hoft (2014-09-04). "ISIS THREATENS PUTIN From Top of Captured Russian

Jet: "We Will Liberate Chechnya & Caucusus" (Video)". The Gateway Pundit.

"Fight against "Islamic State": Bundeswehr flies first military equipment to Iraq". Spiegel Online. 2014-09-05.

"Iraqi and Kurdish troops enter the sieged Amirli". BBC News. Retrieved 31 August 2014.

"So hilft Israels Todfeind den USA im Kampf gegen ISIS!". Bild. Retrieved 4 September 2014.

"In Iraq, residents of Amerli celebrate end of militant siege". The Los Angeles Times. Retrieved 5 September 2014.

http://edition.cnn.com/2014/09/08/world/meast/iraq-town-suicide-bomb-attacks/

Cohen, Tom (10 September 2014). "Obama outlines ISIS strategy: Airstrikes in Syria, more U.S. forces". CNN. Retrieved 10 September 2014.

Masi, Alessandria (12 September 2014). "US-Backed Moderate Group In Syria Signs Truce With ISIS: Reports". International Business Times.

Holmes, Oliver (14 September 2014). "Islamic State video purports to show beheading of UK hostage David Haines". Reuters. Retrieved 14 September 2014.

15 arrested, one charged in terror raids "15 arrested, one charged in terror raids". sbs.com.au. Retrieved 18 September 2014.

"IS leader accused of Sydney terror plot". 7 News. Yahoo7. Retrieved 18 September 2014.

Johnston, Chris (20 September 2014). "Isis militants release 49 hostages taken at Turkish consulate in Mosul".

"ISIS audio urges Muslims everywhere to kill 'unbelievers'". CBC News. Retrieved 22 September 2014.

Cooper, Helene; Schmitt, Eric (22 September 2014). "U.S. and Allies Hit ISIS Targets in Syria". The New York Times. Retrieved 23 September 2014.

"U.S. Military, Partner Nations Conduct Airstrikes Against ISIL in Syria". U.S. Department of Defense (DOD). 23 September 2014. Retrieved 23 September 2014.

"400 ISIL militants killed in int'l alliance attacks". Kuwait News Agency. 23 September 2014. Retrieved 24 September 2014.

www.ingramcontent.com/pod-product-compliance
Lightning Source LLC
Chambersburg PA
CBHW071214280526
45787CB00002B/685